Petra Lihocky

Klett
Grammatik im Griff
Englisch 7./8. Klasse

Mein Übungsbuch für
Gymnasium und Realschule

Klett Lerntraining

Petra Lihocky ist Gymnasiallehrerin für die Fächer Englisch und Deutsch.

Hinweis:
Zu diesem Buch gehören Online-Tests unter
www.klasse5bis10.klett-lerntraining.de.
Der Zugang zu den Online-Abschlusstests ist bis drei Jahre nach Ersterscheinen des Buches gewährleistet.

Bibliografische Information der Deutschen Nationalbibliothek
Die Deutsche Nationalbibliothek verzeichnet diese Publikation in der Deutschen Nationalbibliografie; detaillierte bibliografische Daten sind im Internet über http://dnb.dnb.de abrufbar.

1. Auflage 2018

www.klett-lerntraining.de
Zeichnungen: Kara, Annette Nora, Remseck: 76, 81, 134, 139, 142
Umschlaggestaltung: Sabine Kaufmann, Stuttgart
Umschlagfoto: istockfoto (Viorika), Calgary, Alberta
Außenredaktion: Sabine Schlimm, Hamburg
Satz: DTP-studio Andrea Eckhardt, Göppingen
Druck: medienhaus Plump, Rheinbreitbach
Printed in Germany
ISBN 978-3-12-927417-0

Inhaltsverzeichnis

So übst du mit diesem Buch

Liebe Schülerin, lieber Schüler,

du möchtest fit in der englischen Grammatik werden?
Dann ist „Grammatik im Griff Englisch" genau das richtige Übungsbuch für dich! Es hilft dir dabei, alle **wichtigen Themen** der englischen Grammatik zu wiederholen und zu üben. Gehe so vor:

Schritt 1

Suche aus dem Inhaltsverzeichnis das **Thema heraus**, dass du wiederholen möchtest.

Schritt 2

Lies das **Merkwissen** im Kasten **durch**. Dort steht alles, was du zu diesem Thema wissen und können solltest.

Schritt 3

Jetzt kannst du mit den vielen unterschiedlichen **Aufgaben üben**. Einige Aufgaben lassen sich aus Platzgründen nicht im Buch lösen – lege dir dafür ein Heft zu.

Schritt 4

Vergleiche deine Antworten mit den **Lösungen** hinten im Buch.

Schritt 5

Wenn du ein Kapitel abgeschlossen hast, kannst du dich mit dem **Abschlusstest online testen**. Die Ergebnisse aus dem Test kannst du in die Tabelle am Kapitelende übertragen. So behältst du immer den Überblick.

So funktioniert der Abschlusstest online

Gehe auf **https://www.klett-lerntraining.de/5N5D**.

Du erhältst eine Übersicht über alle Kapitel und darunter alle verfügbaren Abschlusstests.
Wähle einen passenden Test aus und bearbeite die Aufgaben.

Du kannst alle Online-Tests mit und ohne Anmeldung nutzen.
Bitte beachte: Wenn du dich nicht anmeldest, kann dein Lernstand in den Tests **nicht gespeichert** werden.

Eine Anmeldung ist nur möglich, wenn du dich vorher bei uns registriert hast. Dafür musst du dir einen Benutzernamen und ein Passwort ausdenken und deine E-Mail-Adresse angeben. Dann erhältst du einen Aktivierungslink per E-Mail.

Informationen zu Registrierung und Anmeldung findest du immer unter „**Hilfe**" in unserem Lernportal www.klasse5bis10.klett-lerntraining.de.

Viel Erfolg wünschen dir die Autoren und das Team von Klett-Lerntraining

1 Das *present tense*

1.1 Die Formen des *simple present*

Bejahte Formen im *simple present*

Das ***simple present*** ist die einfache Gegenwartsform im Englischen:

	Vollverben	**to be**	**to have got (BE)**	**to have (AE)**
I	play	am	have got	have
you	play	are	have got	have
he/she/it	plays	is	has got	has
we/you/they	play	are	have got	have

To be und *to have got* können auch in der **Kurzform** verwendet werden, z. B. he**'s** (he is)/he**'s got** (he has got). Statt *to have got*, das im britischen Englisch (BE) üblich ist, verwendest du im amerikanischen Englisch (AE) eher *to have* (Kurzform z. B. *he's*, *we've*).

Verneinte Formen im *simple present*

Die Verneinung mit ***to do*** verwendest du, wenn im Satz keine Form von *to be* und keine Hilfsverben, sondern nur Vollverben vorkommen.

	Vollverben	**to be**	**to have got (BE)**	**to have (AE)**
I	do not play	am not	have not got	do not have
you	do not play	are not	have not got	do not have
he/she/it	does not play	is not	has not got	does not have
we/you/they	do not play	are not	have not got	do not have

Die **Kurzformen der Verneinung** lauten:
- doesn't/don't
- isn't/aren't (Ausnahme: I'**m** not)
- hasn't got/haven't got (BE) bzw. doesn't have/don't have (AE)

Entscheidungsfragen und Kurzantworten im *simple present*

Zur Bildung von **Entscheidungsfragen** (auf die du nur mit Ja oder Nein antworten kannst) ziehst du in allen Zeitstufen *to be* oder das Hilfsverb an den Satzanfang (bei Vollverben benutzt du eine Umschreibung mit *to do*). *To be* oder das betreffende Hilfsverb verwendest du auch in der **Kurzantwort**.

Verb	**Frage**	**Bejahte Kurzantwort**	**Verneinte Kurzantwort**
to be	**Is** he ready?	Yes, he **is**.	No, he **isn't**.
to have got (BE)	**Have** you got a key?	Yes, I **have**.	No, I **haven't**.
to have (AE)	**Do** you **have** a key?	Yes, I **have**.	No, I **haven't**.
Vollverb	**Do** they smoke?	Yes, they **do**.	No, they **don't**.
Modalverb	**Can** she swim?	Yes, she **can**.	No, she **can't**.

Ergänzungsfragen im *simple present*

Mit **Ergänzungsfragen** fragst du nach weiteren Informationen. Das Fragewort steht in diesem Fall immer am Anfang der Frage vor der Form von *to be* bzw. dem Hilfsverb. Diese Regel gilt für alle Zeitstufen.

Verb	**Frage**			
to be	Where	**is**	my bag?	
to have got (BE)	What	**have**	you	got?
to have (AE)	What	**do**	you	have?
Vollverb	When	**do**	you	meet?
Modalverb	Why	**must**	they	work?

Sind ***who*** oder ***what*** **Subjekt** des Fragesatzes, ist die Satzstellung identisch mit der des Aussagesatzes. Auch das gilt für alle Zeitstufen.

Emma	walks	to school.
Who	walks	to school?
Dancing	makes	me happy.
What	makes	you happy?

Aufgabe 1: Meet the Sportslovers

Setze die Verben in Klammern im *simple present* in ihrer bejahten oder verneinten Form in die Lücken ein.

a) The Sportslovers ______________________ (be) an American family.

b) They ______________________ (live) in sunny Los Angeles.

c) But they ______________________ (not have) a house in Hollywood.

d) All of them ______________________ (love) sports.

e) They ______________________ (not like) to be lazy (*faul*).

f) Mr Sportslover ______________________ (be) crazy about sailing.

g) He ______________________ (own) a small sailboat (*Segelboot*).

h) Mrs Sportslover ______________________ (play) tennis almost every day.

i) She ______________________ (not need) tennis lessons any more.

j) Their children Emma and Jacob ______________________ (practice) climbing very often.

k) Emma ______________________ (be) Jacob's twin sister (*Zwillingsschwester*).

l) But they ______________________ (not look) alike (gleich).

m) Emma ______________________ (go) swimming in winter and in summer.

n) Jacob ______________________ (have) a very colorful skateboard.

Aufgabe 2: Soccer rules

Bilde Entscheidungsfragen aus den vorgegebenen Sätzen. Antworte mit Ja oder Nein in Form einer Kurzantwort – je nachdem, ob die jeweilige Aussage zum Fußball richtig oder falsch ist.

a) You need eleven players for a soccer team.

Do you need eleven players for a soccer team? Yes, you do.

b) The players use a very big apple as a ball.

c) Each team wants to score as many goals as possible.

d) A goalie's (*Torwart*) job is very important.

e) All goalies are very old.

f) Boys can play better than girls.

g) The soccer referees' whistles (*Trillerpfeifen*) are very loud.

h) Every soccer fan wears a blue scarf.

Aufgabe 3: American football

Frage nach dem unterstrichenen Satzteil.

a) Most Europeans find the rules of American football very difficult.

What do most Europeans find very difficult?

b) You can learn more about these rules in special rule books.

c) Because of the difficult rules the referee needs many helpers.

d) You can see many lines and numbers on a playing field.

e) Before the beginning of each game one team can choose their side of the playing field.

f) The Quarterback is the most important player on a team.

g) He leads the other players.

h) Rugby balls and American footballs look alike (*gleich*) because of their shape.

1.2 Die Formen des *present progressive*

Bejahte und verneinte Formen des *present progressive*

Das ***present progressive*** ist die Verlaufsform der Gegenwart. Sie drückt aus, dass etwas gerade geschieht. Sie wird gebildet aus einer Form von ***to be*** und der ***ing*-Form** (Infinitiv des Vollverbs + *ing*).

I you he/she/it we you they	**am** **are** **is** **are** **are** **are**	(not)	singing

Für die Verneinung setzt du ***not*** nach der Form von *to be* ein. Du kannst auch die entsprechende Kurzform verwenden, z. B. she **isn't** (is not) walking.

Beachte die besondere Schreibung folgender *ing*-Formen:

- Ein stummes e am Wortende fällt weg:
  tak**e** + *ing* → tak**ing**
- Ein Konsonant am Ende des Verbs wird nach einem kurzen, betonten Vokal verdoppelt:
  run + *ing* → run**ning**

Entscheidungsfragen und Kurzantworten im *present progressive*

Zur Bildung von **Entscheidungsfragen** ziehst du die Form von ***to be*** an den Satzanfang. Eine Form von ***to be*** verwendest du auch in der **Kurzantwort**.

Frage	Bejahte Kurzantwort	Verneinte Kurzantwort
Is he crying?	Yes, **he is**.	No, **he isn't**.

Ergänzungsfragen im *present progressive*

In der Regel ziehst du das Fragewort vor die Form von ***to be*** an den Satzanfang (siehe Kapitel 1.1, Seite 9).

Where	**are**	you	driving?

Fragst du allerdings nach dem Subjekt, bleibt die Satzstellung des Aussagesatzes erhalten (siehe Kapitel 1.1, Seite 9):

Emma	is looking	at you.
Who	is looking	at you?

Aufgabe 4: Winter activities

Bilde bejahte oder verneinte Sätze im *present progressive*.

a) they – ski / not swim in the sea

They are skiing. They aren't swimming in the sea.

b) I – have a snowball fight / not eat ice-cream

____

c) she – listen to an audio-book / not dance in an open-air club

____

d) we – drink hot tea / not pick (*pflücken*) fresh fruit

____

e) you – snowboard / not sleep in the sun

____

f) he – sit in front of an open fire / not have a barbecue

____

Aufgabe 5: The Sportslovers' activities

Schreibe auf, was die Personen gerade tun bzw. gerade nicht tun.

a) Mrs Sportslover: play tennis / not sing in a choir

Mrs Sportslover is playing tennis.
She isn't singing in a choir.

b) Emma: fly a kite / not surf the Internet

____

____

c) Mr Sportslover: sail his boat / not make a phone call

____

____

d) Jacob: climb a rock / not run after his sister

____

____

e) Emma and Jacob: practice inline skating / do their homework

____

____

f) Mrs Sportslover: take a break / not prepare dinner

____

____

Aufgabe 6: What are the Sportslovers doing?

Verwende noch einmal die Verben aus Aufgabe 5. Bilde passende Entscheidungsfragen und Kurzantworten und schreibe sie auf.

Beispiel: a) *Is Mrs Sportslover playing tennis? Yes, she is.*
Is she singing in a choir? No, she isn't.

Aufgabe 7: At the fast food restaurant

Was geht im Fast-Food-Restaurant gerade vor? Frage nach dem unterstrichenen Satzteil.

a) Some girls are waiting at the counter.

Where are the girls waiting?

b) A small boy is crying loudly in his father's arms.

c) A young man is preparing burgers in the kitchen.

d) An old woman is washing the dishes.

e) A boy and his sister are having an argument because of the price of the burgers.

f) The manager is giving change to a guest right now.

g) A young woman is cleaning the tables.

h) A family is ordering ice-cold drinks because of the heat.

Aufgabe 8: More about the fast food restaurant

Bringe die Fragen in die richtige Reihenfolge und setze das Verb in Klammern ins *present progressive*.

a) (put) – what – into – she – the salad

b) the ketchup – (get) – he – where

c) (order) – how – he – his lunch

d) they – my fries – when – (bring) – me

e) why – she – (add) – salt – to – her soft drink

f) their chocolate muffins – (have) – when – they

g) he – the guests – how – (talk to)

h) why – (leave) – so much trash (*Abfall*) – on the table – they

1.3 Der Gebrauch von *simple present* und *present progressive*

Die Verwendung des *simple present*

In diesen Fällen verwendest du das *simple present*:

- Etwas ist eine Tatsache:
  Sports **are** good for your health.
- Etwas geschieht häufig, regelmäßig oder aus Gewohnheit:
  I **go** to school every day.
  Signalwörter: *always, sometimes, often, usually, never, every day, every month, every year; on Mondays, on Tuesdays* etc.
- Mehrere Dinge geschehen nacheinander (z. B. in einer Erzählung, Inhaltsangabe oder Anleitung):
  At first David **doesn't play** well. But then he **scores** two goals.
  Signalwörter: *first, then, after that, finally*

Die Verwendung des *present progressive*

In diesen Fällen verwendest du das *present progressive*:

- Etwas geschieht gerade und ist noch nicht abgeschlossen:
  Look, David **is kicking** the ball now.
  Signalwörter: *now, just, at the moment, this morning, this afternoon, this evening, today, look!*

Das musst du außerdem beachten:

- Im Deutschen gibt es keine Verlaufsform. Wir übersetzen die englische Form daher häufig mit „gerade" oder „im Moment":
  John **is practicing** sprints. John **trainiert gerade** Sprints.
- Hilfsverben wie *can, must, to have got* bilden keine Verlaufsform!
- Auch die Verben *to be, to like, to hate* und *to want* werden fast immer im *simple present* verwendet.

Aufgabe 9: Playing a computer game

Setze das *simple present* oder das *present progressive* der angegebenen Verben in die Lücken ein.

a) It ______________________________ (rain) really hard outside this afternoon.

b) Look, Emma and Jacob ______________________________ (play) a computer game.

c) They ______________________________ (like) that game very much.

d) It ______________________________ (be) about adventures (*Abenteuer*) on a lonely island.

e) The players ______________________________ (must) find a hidden treasure.

f) But a few pirates ______________________________ (want) to find the treasure, too.

g) Emma ______________________________ (fight) a pirate now.

h) Oh no, Emma ______________________________ (have) bad luck today!

i) She ______________________________ (lose) against the strong pirate!

j) Emma ______________________________ (hate) losing.

k) Jacob ______________________________ (want) to play next.

l) He ______________________________ (not can) wait to start his adventure.

Aufgabe 10: Chaos at the zoo

Im Zoo von Los Angeles geht heute alles drunter und drüber. Setze das *simple present* oder das *present progressive* der angegebenen Verben in die Lücken ein.

a) Usually there ______________________ (be) only a few visitors at the zoo on Monday mornings.

b) But it seems hundreds of students ______________________ (run) around there right now.

c) Normally the old brown bear (*Bär*) ______________________ (sleep) the whole day.

d) But right now it is ______________________ (dance) around nervously in its cage (*Käfig*).

e) Usually children ______________________ (can) feed the ponies without any problems.

f) But look, one of the ponies ______________________ (try) to bite a little boy's hand!

g) Over there, a small wolf ______________________ (now – chase) its brother.

h) That is strange, as they normally ______________________ (play) together peacefully (*friedlich*).

i) Everybody knows that monkeys ______________________ (like) lots of bananas.

j) But today they ______________________ (not eat) their bananas.

k) Look, they ______________________ (throw) them out of their cages!

Abschlusstest online 1

Herzlichen Glückwunsch! Du hast das **Kapitel 1 – Das *present tense*** durchgearbeitet. Jetzt weißt du wieder ganz genau, wie man im Englischen die Gegenwart beschreibt: nämlich je nachdem, ob etwas gerade im Moment passiert (*present progressive*) oder ob du über etwas berichtest, das regelmäßig abläuft oder allgemeingültig ist (*simple present*).

So funktioniert der Abschlusstest online:
Um deinen Lernerfolg zu überprüfen, kannst du nun die Abschlusstests machen. Gehe auf
https://www.klett-lerntraining.de/5N5D
und wähle das Kapitel und einen Test aus.

Welche Tests es gibt, siehst du unten in der Tabelle. Nach jedem Test bekommst du eine Auswertung.

Willst du immer im Blick haben, welche Themen du schon kannst oder was du besser wiederholen solltest? Dann schreibe deine Ergebnisse in die Tabelle.

Mein Ergebnis im Abschlusstest online – Kapitel 1

Thema	Mein Ergebnis
Die Formen des *simple present*	
Die Formen des *present progressive*	
Der Gebrauch von *simple present* und *present progressive*	

2 Das *past tense*

2.1 Die Formen des *simple past*

Bejahte Formen im *simple past*

Die einfache Form der Vergangenheit, das ***simple past***, verwendest du, wenn du über abgeschlossene Vorgänge in der Vergangenheit sprichst.

Bei den **regelmäßigen Verben** (*regular verbs*) hängst du die Endung **ed** an den Infinitiv an:
play + ed → played

Einige Verben bilden das simple past **unregelmäßig** (*irregular verbs*), wie z. B. make → **made**. Diese Formen musst du lernen. Ein Verzeichnis findest du in deinem Englischbuch.

Die Formen des *simple past* lauten für alle Personen gleich, bei regelmäßigen wie bei unregelmäßigen Verben. Die einzige Ausnahme ist das Verb ***to be***:

	Vollverben	**to be**
I you he/she/it we/you/they	played	was were was were

Regeln zur Schreibung der regelmäßigen Verben:

- Ein **stummes e** am Ende des Verbs fällt weg:
  lik**e** + ed → liked
- Nach Konsonant + y am Wortende wird y zu **i**:
  tr**y** + ed → tr**i**ed
- Ein Konsonant am Wortende, der nach einem betonten Kurzvokal steht, verdoppelt sich:
  sto**p** + ed → sto**pp**ed

Verneinte Formen im *simple past*

Vollverben (außer *to be*) verneinst du im *simple past*, indem du ***did not*** einfügst, die *simple-past*-Form von *do not/does not*. Das Vollverb steht im Infinitiv.

Zur Verneinung von ***to be*** brauchst du keine Umschreibung mit *did not*. Du setzt einfach ***not*** nach der entsprechenden Form von ***to be*** ein:

	Vollverben	**to be**
I you he/she/it we/you/they	did not play	**was not** **were not** **was not** **were not**

Du kannst auch **Kurzformen** benutzen:
did not → didn't   *was not → wasn't*   *were not → weren't*

Entscheidungsfragen und Kurzantworten im *simple past*

Das Hilfsverb steht bei Entscheidungsfragen am Satzanfang:

Verb	**Frage**	**Bejahte Kurzantwort**	**Verneinte Kurzantwort**
to be	**Were you** there?	Yes, **I was**.	No, **I wasn't**.
Vollverb	**Did he** walk?	Yes, **he did**.	No, **he didn't**.

Ergänzungsfragen im *simple past*

Bei Fragen nach dem Objekt/der adverbialen Bestimmung steht das Fragewort vor dem Hilfsverb bzw. der Form von *to be* am Anfang des Satzes (siehe Kapitel 1.1, Seite 9):

Verb	**Frage**			
to be	**Where**	**were**	you?	
Vollverb	**When**	**did**	he	arrive?

Bei Fragen nach dem Subjekt bleibt die Satzstellung des Aussagesatzes erhalten (siehe Kapitel 1.1, Seite 9).

Aufgabe 1: A boat trip

In dem Rätsel sind zehn Verben waagerecht, senkrecht oder quer (auch rückwärts) versteckt. Hast du sie gefunden? Dann musst du sie nur noch im *simple past* in die richtige Lücke setzen!

t _ _ _ , c _ _ _ _ _ , h _ _ _ , g _ , b _ , s _ _ _ _ _ , m _ _ _ , b _ _ _ _ _ , e _ _ ,

g e t u p

J	E	V	A	H	G	B	P
A	H	C	J	O	H	E	D
S	C	E	D	N	E	P	S
B	T	B	K	J	I	W	**G**
E	A	Q	E	A	W	Z	**E**
K	C	R	O	G	M	C	**T**
A	H	C	F	S	I	K	**U**
T	L	F	T	A	E	N	**P**

a) Last Sunday Emma and Jacob got up very early.

b) They ________________ a boat trip with their parents.

c) The family ________________ their trip before sunrise (*Sonnenaufgang*).

d) All of them ________________ still a little tired.

e) First they ________________ breakfast on the boat together.

f) Each of them ________________ a big bowl of cornflakes.

g) Later Emma and Jacob ________________ into the water for a swim.

h) Jacob and his father ________________ some fish.

i) So Emma ________________ a nice fish soup for dinner.

j) The Sportslovers ________________ the whole day at sea.

Aufgabe 2: Finding opposites

In der Wörterschlange sind fünf Verbpaare im Infinitiv versteckt. Schreibe sie auf und setze sie anschließend ins *simple past*.

winbalosekirememberpnforgetxrgivevmkeepcafindnihiderecomehuleave

Aufgabe 3: Sports in the past

Setze die in Klammern angegebenen Verben in die bejahte oder verneinte Form des *simple past*.

a) In the 19th century sportsmen ______________________________ (not wear) plastic shoes.

b) They only ______________________________ (wear) leather shoes.

c) In the 1950s some professional athletes (*Sportler*) ______________________________ (not earn) any money.

d) Most of them ______________________________ (earn) much less than today's successful athletes.

e) A hundred years ago bikes ______________________________ (not be) as lightweight (*leicht*) as today.

f) A bike ______________________________ (be) also much slower than today's bikes are.

g) Fifty years ago soccer clubs only ______________________________ (sell) a few fan articles.

h) They ______________________________ (not sell) as many T-shirts and scarves as today's big soccer clubs.

Aufgabe 4: At the movie studios

Emma und Jacob haben eine Cousine in Deutschland. In dieser Übung erfährst du, was Lena und ihre Eltern bei ihrem Besuch in LA erlebt haben. Setze dazu die in Klammern angegebenen Verben in die bejahte oder verneinte Form des *simple past*.

a) Lena and her parents ______________________ (fly) from Frankfurt to Los Angeles last summer.

b) They ______________________ (want) to stay there for a few days.

c) At first Lena ______________________ (not understand) a lot of English.

d) But she ______________________ (feel) excited about being in the movie capital (*Hauptstadt*) of the world.

e) On the third day of their vacation, Lena and her parents ______________________ (visit) a few famous movie studios.

f) The tickets ______________________ (not be) very cheap.

g) Lena ______________________ (be) disappointed (*enttäuscht*) …

h) … because she ______________________ (not meet) any movie stars there.

i) She ______________________ (not talk) to any famous people.

j) But Lena and her parents ______________________ (learn) a lot about special effects that day.

Aufgabe 5: Questions to Lena

Emma und Jacob stellen Lena nach ihrem Besuch in den Filmstudios viele Fragen. Schreibe diese zusammen mit Lenas kurzen Antworten im *simple past* in die entsprechenden Lücken.

a) Were (there – be) many other tourists at the movie studios?

Yes, there were.

b) ______________________ (you – buy) any souvenirs?

No, ______________________.

c) ______________________ (you – see) a stuntman?

Yes, ______________________.

d) ______________________ (he – perform) any stunts for you and the other visitors? – Yes, ______________________.

e) ______________________ (your parents – take) any pictures at the studios? – No, ______________________.

f) ______________________ (you all – enjoy) the tour?

Yes, ______________________.

Aufgabe 6: Emma in trouble

Emma ist zu spät von einer Party nach Hause gekommen. Ihre Eltern stellen ihr deshalb am nächsten Morgen einige Fragen. Schreibe die Fragen im *simple past* und in der richtigen Reihenfolge auf.

a) the party – why – (leave) – you – later than your brother

b) (drink) – what – at that party – you

c) such a short skirt – you – why – (wear)

d) (not call) – us – you – from the party – why

e) in the middle of the night – home – you – how – (get)

2.2 Die Formen des *past progressive*

Bejahte und verneinte Formen des *past progressive*

Die Verlaufsform der Vergangenheit, das ***past progressive***, drückt aus, dass eine Handlung zu einem bestimmten Zeitpunkt in der Vergangenheit noch andauerte.

Genau wie das *present progressive* bildet man das ***past progressive*** aus einer Form von ***to be***, in diesem Fall ***was/were***, und der ***ing***-Form.

I you he/she/it we/you/they	**was** **were** **was** **were**	**(not)**	**listening**

Für die Verneinung setzt du ***not*** nach *was/were* ein. Du kannst auch die entsprechenden Kurzformen *wasn't* oder *weren't* verwenden.

Entscheidungsfragen und Kurzantworten im *past progressive*

Für **Entscheidungsfragen** ziehst du *was* oder *were* an den Satzanfang. Auch die **Kurzantwort** bildest du mit *was/were:*

Frage	Bejahte Kurzantwort	Verneinte Kurzantwort
Was he singing?	Yes, **he was**.	No, **he wasn't**.

Ergänzungsfragen im *past progressive*

Bei Fragen nach dem Objekt oder der adverbialen Bestimmung (siehe Kapitel 1.1, Seite 9) steht das Fragewort vor *was/were* am Satzanfang:

Frage			
Why	**were**	you	sleeping?

Bei Fragen nach dem Subjekt bleibt die Satzstellung des Aussagesatzes erhalten (siehe Kapitel 1.1, Seite 9).

Emma	was dancing.
Who	was dancing?

Aufgabe 7: Visiting Venice Beach

Auf der Strandpromenade von Venice Beach in Los Angeles war gestern Nachmittag viel los. Schreibe auf, was die Leute gerade machten bzw. nicht machten, als Emma dort vorbeikam.

a) an artist: paint a portrait / not do aerobics

An artist was painting a portrait.
He / She wasn't doing aerobics.

b) a young woman: juggle (*jonglieren*) balls / not take a dog for a walk

____

____

c) a young man: blow fire (*Feuer schlucken*) / not go shopping

____

____

d) a street musician: play the guitar / not hold an umbrella

____

____

e) a comedian: tell jokes / not take notes

____

____

f) two boys: breakdance / not wear goggles

____

____

Aufgabe 8: What was happening at Venice Beach?

Verwende noch einmal die Angaben aus Aufgabe 7. Bilde passende Entscheidungsfragen und Kurzantworten.

Beispiel: a) *Was the artist painting a portrait? Yes, he was.*
Was he doing aerobics? No, he wasn't.

Aufgabe 9: More activities at Venice Beach

Setze die in Klammern angegebenen Verben ins *past progressive*. (Die Unterstreichungen brauchst du dabei erst einmal nicht zu beachten.)

a) An old woman ______________________________ (read) the future in a young girl's hand.

b) Two teenagers ______________________________ (paint) graffiti on a wall.

c) At a beach bar a policeman ______________________________ (watch) the crowd.

d) I ______________________________ (chat) to a surfing instructor (*Surflehrer*) because of my interest in surfing.

e) A boy ______________________________ (do) tricks on his skateboard.

f) A few girls ______________________________ (sell) colorful jewelry.

g) A street musician ______________________________ (play) for money in front of a café.

h) You ______________________________ (look) for a place to sit at the waterfront.

i) A pickpocket (*Taschendieb*) ______________________________ (steal) a woman's purse.

j) A dog ______________________________ (sit) in the shade (*Schatten*) because of the heat.

Aufgabe 10: What else?

Benutze noch einmal die Sätze aus Aufgabe 9. Frage nun jeweils nach dem unterstrichenen Satzteil.

Beispiel: a) *What was the old woman reading in the young girl's hand?*

Aufgabe 11: A normal lesson?

Bilde mithilfe der Angaben in Klammern Aussagesätze und Fragen im *past progressive*.

a) While ____

(Emma's teacher – write) a few grammar rules on the board …

b) … ____

(only some of the students – copy) the rules into their exercise books.

c) What ____

______________________ (all the other students – do)?

d) How ____

______________________ (they – spend) their time?

e) ______________________ (why – Cathy and Zoey – not listen) to the teacher's explanations (*Erklärungen*)?

f) ____

______________________ (they – have) an argument.

g) ____

______________________ (Josh – use) his cell phone (*Handy*)?

h) Yes, ____

______________________ (he – text) his girlfriend.

i) ____

______________________ (why – Miles – crawl: *kriechen*) under his desk?

j) ____

(he – look for) his pen.

2.3 Der Gebrauch von *simple past* und *past progressive*

Die Verwendung des *simple past*

- Mit dem *simple past* kannst du über abgeschlossene Handlungen in der Vergangenheit erzählen oder berichten.
  Emma and Jacob **had** an argument **yesterday**.
  Signalwörter: *yesterday, last week, last year, in the morning, in the evening* etc.
  Auch *when* ist ein Signalwort für das *simple past*, es leitet Nebensätze ein:
  When Jacob **apologized** to Emma, she **was** still angry at him.

Die Verwendung des *past progressive*

- Das *past progressive* betont die Dauer einer vergangenen Handlung.
  Jacob **was rock climbing** all day.
- Es wird verwendet für Handlungen, die zu einem bestimmten Zeitpunkt in der Vergangenheit andauerten und noch nicht abgeschlossen waren.
  At 10 pm Emma **was traveling** home.
- Das *past progressive* betont, dass eine Handlung noch andauerte, während eine neue Handlung einsetzte. Diese neue Handlung steht im *simple past*.
  Emma **was** just **cycling** home when her cell phone (*Handy*) rang.
  Signalwörter: *still, just, while*

Das musst du außerdem beachten:

- Hilfsverben wie *can, must, to have* (*got*) bilden keine Verlaufsform!
- Auch die Verben *to be, to like, to hate* und *to want* werden fast immer im *simple past* verwendet.

Aufgabe 12: A strange guest (Gast)

Ergänze die Sätze mithilfe der in Klammern angegebenen Wörter. Setze die Verben ins *simple past* oder *past progressive*.

a) Last Sunday something strange ________________________________

(happen) in the Sportslovers' neighborhood (*Nachbarschaft*).

b) An old lady ____
(just – have) a cup of coffee in her kitchen …

c) … when she ____ (hear)
a loud noise from her garden.

d) So she ____ (quickly – go)
outside.

e) A surprise ____
(already – wait) for her under her sunshade (*Sonnenschirm*).

f) A small brown kangaroo (*Känguru*)
____ (enjoying) a meal
of grass and fresh leaves (*Blätter*).

g) At first the old lady
____ (be) too shocked
to act.

h) Then she ____ (take)
her phone to call the police.

i) Ten minutes later a big car with two policemen and a zoo keeper (*Wärter*)
____ (arrive).

j) While the zoo keeper
____ (offer) the
kangaroo some fruit …

k) … the two policemen
____ (try) to catch the
animal with a rope (*Seil*).

l) Finally they ____ (manage)
to take the kangaroo back to the zoo.

Aufgabe 13: Mia's little charm (*Glücksbringer*)

Jemand hat Mias Glücksbringer aus ihrer Tasche im Klassenzimmer gestohlen. Es handelt sich um eine kleine Schildkröte *(turtle)* aus Holz. Der Klassenlehrer befragt Mia, um Genaueres herauszufinden. Bilde Aussagesätze oder Fragen im *simple past* oder *past progressive* mithilfe der Angaben in Klammern!

a) Teacher: "____

(when – little turtle – disappear), Mia?"

b) Mia: "____ (it – sit)

on my desk during the English test before the lunch break.

c) When ____ (the test –

be) over, …

d) … ____ (I – put) it

back into my bag.

e) Then ____ (I – go)

to the school cafeteria …

f) … and ____ (leave)

my bag in the classroom."

g) Teacher: "____

(anybody – stay) in the classroom during the lunch break?"

h) Mia: "Yes, ____

(Ava and Grace – listen) to music on Ava's cell phone (*Handy*).

i) And ____

(Anthony – sleep) at his desk, I think."

j) Teacher: "So ____

(he – not can) see …

k) who ____ (do) what."

Abschlusstest online 2

Super! Nachdem du das **Kapitel 2 – Das *past tense*** durchgearbeitet hast, weißt du wieder, wie du über die Vergangenheit berichten kannst. Auch dazu hast du zwei Möglichkeiten: das *simple past* für abgeschlossene Handlungen und das *past progressive* für Handlungen, die zu einem bestimmten Zeitpunkt in der Vergangenheit immer noch andauerten.

So funktioniert der Abschlusstest online:
Um deinen Lernerfolg zu überprüfen, kannst du nun die Abschlusstests machen. Gehe auf
https://www.klett-lerntraining.de/5N5D
und wähle das Kapitel und einen Test aus.

Welche Tests es gibt, siehst du unten in der Tabelle. Nach jedem Test bekommst du eine Auswertung.

Willst du immer im Blick haben, welche Themen du schon kannst oder was du besser wiederholen solltest? Dann schreibe deine Ergebnisse in die Tabelle.

Mein Ergebnis im Abschlusstest online – Kapitel 2

Thema	Mein Ergebnis
Die Formen des *simple past*	
Die Formen des *past progressive*	
Der Gebrauch von *simple past* und *past progressive*	

3 Das *present perfect*

3.1 Die Formen des (*simple*) *present perfect*

Das ***present perfect*** drückt aus, dass etwas in der Vergangenheit geschehen ist, die Auswirkungen oder Ergebnisse aber noch spürbar sind. Außerdem wird es verwendet, wenn eine Handlung gerade erst abgeschlossen wurde.
Für die Bildung brauchst du das ***past participle***.

Das *past participle* regelmäßiger und unregelmäßiger Verben

Bei **regelmäßigen Verben** (*regular verbs*) wird das ***past participle*** wie das *simple past* aus dem **Infinitiv des Verbs + ed** gebildet:
play + ed → play**ed**

Besonderheiten zur Schreibung findest du in Kapitel 2.1, Seite 20.

Die Formen der **unregelmäßigen Verben** (*irregular verbs*), z. B. make → **made**, musst du auswendig lernen.

Bejahte und verneinte Formen des (*simple*) *present perfect*

Das ***present perfect*** wird aus ***have*/*has*** und dem ***past participle*** gebildet.

I you he/she/it we/you/they	**have** **have** **has** **have**	**(not)**	**played**

Die **Verneinung** bildest du, indem du ***not*** nach *have*/*has* einsetzt.

Du kannst auch die entsprechenden Kurzformen verwenden:
I'**ve** talked to my friend. He'**s** played a computer game.
I **haven't** bought any cheese. He **hasn't** had lunch yet.

Entscheidungsfragen im (*simple*) *present perfect*

Für **Entscheidungsfragen** ziehst du ***have*** oder ***has*** an den Satzanfang.
Auch die **Kurzantwort** bildest du mit ***have*/*has***:

Frage	Bejahte Kurzantwort	Verneinte Kurzantwort
Has he seen … ?	Yes, **he has.**	No, **he hasn't.**

Ergänzungsfragen im (*simple*) *present perfect*

Bei Fragen nach dem Objekt/der adverbialen Bestimmung steht das Fragewort vor ***have*/*has*** am Anfang des Satzes (siehe Kapitel 1.1, Seite 9):

What	has	he	written	so far?

Bei Fragen nach dem Subjekt bleibt die Satzstellung des Aussagesatzes erhalten (siehe Kapitel 1.1, Seite 9).

Emma	has	eaten	all the cookies.
Who	has	eaten	all the cookies?

Die Satzstellung im (*simple*) *present perfect*

- Anders als im Deutschen steht im Englischen das *past participle* immer vor dem Objekt. Das gilt für Aussagesätze und Fragen.

Emma	has	**shown**	Jacob	a picture.	
Emma	hat		Jacob	ein Bild	**gezeigt**.

- Die **Signalwörter** *just*, *already*, *ever*, *never* stehen in Aussagesätzen und Fragen vor dem *past participle*.

	Jacob	has	**just/already/never**	read	this book.
Has	he		**ever**	seen	this film?

- Mit *not … yet* drückst du aus, dass etwas noch nicht geschehen ist.
  Das **Signalwort** *yet* steht hierbei am Satzende:
  We haven't met her **yet**.

Aufgabe 1: Good luck!

Setze die in Klammern angegebenen Verben ins *present perfect*. Achte auf die richtige Stellung der Adverbien.

a) He ____

(just – choose) the numbers for the lottery (*Lotto*).

b) She ____

(already – get) a call from the nice boy she met at the party yesterday.

c) You ____

(never – have) bad weather while you were on vacation (*Urlaub*).

d) They ____

(just – find) the house of their dreams.

e) I ____

(never – lose) a friend.

f) You ____

(already – sort out) your problem.

Aufgabe 2: Open day

Für den Tag der offenen Tür an Emmas und Jacobs Schule sind noch viele Vorbereitungen zu treffen. Bilde mithilfe der vorgegebenen Stichworte Fragesätze mit *already* und Antworten mit *not yet*.

a) school band – practice all the songs for the concert

Has the school band already practiced all the songs for the concert?
No, it hasn't practiced all the songs for the concert yet.

b) students – make all the posters for the school hall

c) headmaster – write down the program

d) janitor (*Hausmeister*) – repair all the broken chairs

e) school secretary – send invitations to all students' families

f) teachers – finish all the class projects

Aufgabe 3: Before the basketball game

Bilde mithilfe der in Klammern angegebenen Wörter Aussagesätze, Entscheidungsfragen, Kurzantworten oder Ergänzungsfragen im *present perfect*. Achte auf die richtige Wortstellung.

a) The Sportslovers are really lucky.

What ______________________________ (happen)?

b) ______________________________

(they – just – buy) tickets to a basketball game to see their favorite team.

c) ______________________________

(they – ever – see) a game with this team before? –

Yes, ______________________________.

d) ______________________________

(they– ever – wear) their fan shirts before? –

No, ______________________________.

e) ______________________________

(they – already – sit down) in the stadium? –

No, ______________________________.

f) Why ______________________________

(they – not find) their seats yet?

g) ______________________________

(they – get lost) in the stadium? –

No, ______________________________.

h) ______________________________

(they – just – have) an interesting conversation.

i) Who ______________________________

(they – just – talk) to?

j) ______________________________

(they – just – speak) with the team's captain.

3.2 Die Formen des *present perfect progressive*

Das ***present perfect progressive*** verwendest du für Handlungen, die in der Vergangenheit begonnen haben und bis jetzt andauern.

Bejahte und verneinte Formen des *present perfect progressive*

Das *present perfect progressive* wird aus ***have been*/*has been*** und der ***ing***-Form gebildet.

I you he/she/it we you they	**have** **have** **has** **have** **have** **have**	**(not)**	**been**	**playing**

Die **Verneinung** bildest du, indem du ***not*** nach *have*/*has* einsetzt.
Du kannst in bejahten und verneinten Sätzen auch die entsprechenden **Kurzformen** verwenden:

I**'ve** been waiting for 3 hours.
I **haven't** been watching TV.

It**'s** been raining all day.
He **hasn't** been sleeping a long time.

Entscheidungsfragen und Kurzantworten im *present perfect progressive*

Für **Entscheidungsfragen** ziehst du ***have*** oder ***has*** an den Satzanfang.
Auch die **Kurzantwort** bildest du mit ***have*/*has***:

Frage	Bejahte Kurzantwort	Verneinte Kurzantwort
Has he been waiting?	Yes, **he has**.	No, **he hasn't**.

Ergänzungsfragen im *present perfect progressive*

Bei Fragen nach dem Objekt/der adverbialen Bestimmung steht das Fragewort vor ***have*/*has*** am Anfang des Satzes (siehe Kapitel 1.1, Seite 9):

What	has	he	been doing	all morning?

Bei Fragen nach dem Subjekt bleibt die Satzstellung des Aussagesatzes erhalten (siehe Kapitel 1.1, Seite 9):

He	has	been	standing	in the rain.
Who	has	been	standing	in the rain?

Aufgabe 4: At the hotel

Viele Gäste im Hotel beschweren sich. Suche ein passendes Verb aus und setze es im *present perfect progressive* in die Lücke ein.

ring – look for – run – listen to – try – wait

a) I ________________________________ for a drink at the hotel bar all night.

b) My husband ________________________________ the bell at the reception for the last fifteen minutes.

c) My wife ________________________________ to order something from room service since midnight.

d) We ________________________________ the price list of the mini bar all evening.

e) The shower ________________________________ for half an hour, but the water is still cold.

f) My mother can't sleep. She ________________________________ the party in the room next door for hours.

Aufgabe 5: Flirting lessons

Hier geht es um Sprüche, die manchmal verwendet werden, um ein Mädchen oder einen Jungen z. B. auf einer Party anzusprechen. Setze die in Klammern angegebenen Verben ins *present perfect progressive* und suche eine passende Zeitangabe aus. Wenn du Lust hast, wähle am Ende den schlechtesten und den besten Spruch aus.

for hours – all my life – for too long – all night – since the beginning of the party – for ages – the whole evening – for years

a) You ______________________ (try) to get my attention ______________________, haven't you?

b) I ______________________ (not look) at anyone but you ______________________.

c) You ______________________ (dance) with the wrong partners ______________________. Come and dance with me!

d) I ______________________ (dream) of someone like you ______________________.

e) You ______________________ (think) of coming over to our table ______________________, haven't you?

f) I ______________________ (admire) your T-shirt ______________________.

g) You ______________________ (stand) here on your own ______________________. Would you like to have some company (*Gesellschaft*)?

h) I ______________________ (search) for the perfect girl/boy ______________________. My search is over now!

Aufgabe 6: A perfect date?

Emma hat eine Verabredung mit einem Jungen names Alec. Nicht alles verläuft so, wie sie sich das vorgestellt hat … Bilde mithilfe der in Klammern angegebenen Wörter Aussagesätze, Entscheidungsfragen, Kurzantworten oder Ergänzungsfragen im *present perfect progressive*. Achte auf die richtige Wortstellung.

a) What ____________________

(Emma and Alec – do) all evening?

b) Where ____________________

(they – spend) their time together?

c) ____________________

(they – walk) along the beach? – No, ____________________

____________________.

d) ____________________

(they – look) at the stars? – No, ____________________

____________________.

e) ____________________ (they – watch)

a movie? – No, ____________________.

f) ____________________ (they – spend)

their time at a shopping mall.

g) ____________________ (Alec – hold)

Emma's hand? – No, ____________________.

h) ____________________ (he – carry)

around his laptop and a bottle of coke.

i) What ____________________ (Emma and Alec – talk)

about for the last hour?

j) ____________________ (Alec – tell)

Emma jokes which aren't funny.

3.3 Der Gebrauch von *since* und *for*

Since und ***for*** werden sehr häufig mit dem ***present perfect progressive*** verwendet, können aber auch mit dem einfachen **(*simple*)** ***present perfect*** stehen.

<table>
<tr><th>since</th><th>for</th></tr>
<tr><td>Since bezieht sich auf den Zeitpunkt, an dem eine Handlung oder ein Zustand begonnen hat:

Since steht mit einer Uhrzeit, einem Datum, einem bestimmten Tag oder einem bestimmten Jahr.</td><td>For bezieht sich auf den Zeitraum, den eine Handlung oder ein Zustand (schon) andauert:
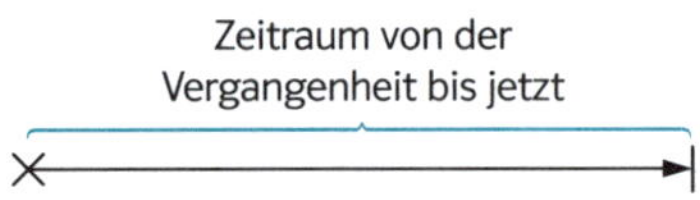

For steht mit Ausdrücken wie (two) hours, (many) days, (three) years, a long time etc.</td></tr>
<tr><td colspan="2">Achtung: Sätze mit since und for werden im Deutschen oft in der Gegenwart wiedergegeben!</td></tr>
<tr><td>I have lived here since 2010.
Ich lebe hier (schon) seit 2010.

She has been sleeping since 9 o'clock.
Sie schläft (schon) seit 9 Uhr.</td><td>We have been here for days.
Wir sind schon seit Tagen hier.

I have been learning English for three years.
Ich lerne (schon) seit drei Jahren Englisch.</td></tr>
</table>

Der Zeitpunkt, auf den sich ***since*** bezieht, kann auch in Form eines **Nebensatzes im *simple past*** angegeben werden. Dieser Nebensatz bezeichnet dann ein vergangenes, abgeschlossenes Ereignis:

We **have been walking** since we **got off** the bus.

Aufgabe 7: Since or for?

Setze *for* oder *since* in die Lücken ein.

a) ____________ last Monday
b) ____________ yesterday
c) ____________ twenty minutes
d) ____________ my whole life
e) ____________ a couple of weeks
f) ____________ a few months
g) ____________ the year 2012
h) ____________ I was born

Aufgabe 8: They are all angry

Alle Mitglieder der Familie Sportslover ärgern sich über irgendetwas. Suche die passenden Verbformen aus und setze sie ein.

has been trying – sent – has been standing – hasn't heard – ordered – got up – hasn't arrived – started – met – has been waiting – phoned – hasn't got

a) Emma ________________________________ for a reply (*Antwort*) to her mail since she ________________________________ it last December.

b) The taxi ________________________________ even though (*obwohl*) the Sportslovers ________________________________ for it forty minutes ago.

c) Jacob ________________________________ to call his friend since he ________________________________ in the early morning.

d) Mrs Sportslover ________________________________ from her friend Amy since they ________________________________ for lunch a year ago.

e) Mr Sportslover ________________________________ anything to eat even though he ________________________________ the food two hours ago.

f) Emma ________________________________ at the bus stop since it ________________________________ raining.

3.4 Der Gebrauch von (*simple*) *present perfect*, *present perfect progressive* und *simple past*

In diesen Fällen verwendest du das (*simple*) *present perfect*:

- Wenn Handlungen in der Vergangenheit stattfanden, ihre Auswirkung aber in der Gegenwart spürbar ist.
  She **has lost** her keys.
  → Sie steht vor der Tür und kommt nicht hinein.
- Wenn Handlungen gerade erst abgeschlossen wurden.
  The audience **has** just **seen** a very good film.
  Signalwort: *just*
- Wenn du betonst, dass etwas Bestimmtes in einem Zeitraum, der bis in die Gegenwart reicht, geschehen (oder nicht geschehen) ist. Entscheidend ist das Ereignis, nicht die Dauer.
  The actor **has** never **read** such a good script.
  Signalwörter: *already, ever, never, so far, yet*

In diesen Fällen verwendest du das *present perfect progressive*:

- Wenn du die Dauer einer Handlung betonst, die in der Vergangenheit begonnen hat und noch nicht beendet ist.
  She **has been waiting** for hours.
  Signalwörter: *since, for*
- **Achtung**: Hilfsverben wie *can, must, to have got* bilden keine Verlaufsform! Auch die Verben *to be, to like, to hate* und *to want* werden in der Regel nicht im *present perfect progressive* verwendet.

In diesen Fällen verwendest du das *simple past*:

- Wenn du über abgeschlossene Handlungen in der Vergangenheit redest. Häufig nennst du gleichzeitig einen bestimmten Zeitpunkt.
  The actress **came** to Hollywood when she was eighteen.
  Signalwörter: *yesterday, last week, last year, in the morning, in the evening*; *when* (zur Einleitung von Nebensätzen)

Beachte die Unterschiede zwischen der Zeitenverwendung im Deutschen und Englischen:

- Das deutsche Perfekt musst du häufig (aber nicht immer!) als *simple past* übersetzen:
  Sie **hat** gestern ein Filmstudio **besucht**.
  She **visited** a movie studio **yesterday**. **(Signalwort!)**
- Das deutsche Präsens hingegen musst du manchmal mit dem *present perfect* wiedergeben:
  Dieses Kino **gibt** es schon seit zehn Jahren.
  This cinema **has been** there for ten years. **(Signalwort!)**

Aufgabe 9: Say it in English

Vervollständige die englische Übersetzung der deutschen Sätze.

a) Das Basketballspiel hat um fünfzehn Uhr begonnen.

The basketball game ______________________________ at 3 pm.

b) Es dauert schon über eine Stunde.

It ______________________________ for more than an hour.

c) Beide Mannschaften haben schon viele Punkte erzielt.

Both teams ______________________________ many points.

d) Erst vor einer Woche haben die beiden Mannschaften gegeneinander gespielt.

Only a week ago the two teams ______________________________ against each other.

e) Bisher ist das Publikum sehr zufrieden mit dem Spiel.

Up to now the audience ______________________________ very happy with the game.

Aufgabe 10: Exploring space

Setze die in Klammern angegebenen Verben in die richtige Form: *simple past*, (*simple*) *present perfect* oder *present perfect progressive*?

a) Since scientists ______________________
(send) the first satellite into space …

b) … there ______________________ (be) a lot of
progress (*Fortschritt*) in space technology.

c) Astronauts (*Astronauten*) ______________________
(land) on the moon for the first time in 1969.

d) Since then scientists ______________________
(dream) of sending spaceships with astronauts to Mars.

e) Astronauts ______________________ (do)
many experiments (*Experimente*) with plants and animals in space over the last several (*etliche*) years.

f) But people ______________________ (not
discover) a way to survive in space for longer journeys of four or five years yet.

g) Satellites ______________________ (play)
a very important role in daily life for many years.

h) People ______________________
(only – not use) them to get information about the weather.

i) Satellites ______________________
(also – help) drivers to find their way or to avoid traffic jams (*Staus*).

j) In the 1950s, nobody ______________________
(imagine) that space technology would become such a normal part of life.

Abschlusstest online 3

Großartig! Du hast das **Kapitel 3 – Das *present perfect*** durchgearbeitet. Dabei konntest du dir noch einmal ins Gedächtnis rufen, dass es im Englischen eine eigene Form gibt, über etwas zu sprechen, das gerade erst vergangen ist oder dessen Nachwirkungen noch spürbar sind: das *present perfect*. Und wie im Englischen üblich, gibt es diese Zeit in einer *simple*- und einer *progressive*-Form.

So funktioniert der Abschlusstest online:
Um deinen Lernerfolg zu überprüfen, kannst du nun die Abschlusstests machen. Gehe auf
https://www.klett-lerntraining.de/5N5D
und wähle das Kapitel und einen Test aus.

Welche Tests es gibt, siehst du unten in der Tabelle. Nach jedem Test bekommst du eine Auswertung.

Willst du immer im Blick haben, welche Themen du schon kannst oder was du besser wiederholen solltest? Dann schreibe deine Ergebnisse in die Tabelle.

Mein Ergebnis im Abschlusstest online – Kapitel 3

Thema	Mein Ergebnis
Die Formen des (*simple*) *present perfect*	
Die Formen des *present perfect progressive*	
Der Gebrauch von *since* und *for*	
Der Gebrauch von (*simple*) *present perfect*, *present perfect progressive* und *simple past*	

4 Das *past perfect*

4.1 Die Formen des (*simple*) *past perfect*

Um über abgeschlossene Handlungen in der Vergangenheit zu sprechen, verwendest du das *simple past*. Mit dem (***simple***) ***past perfect*** betonst du, dass ein Ereignis noch **vor** einem anderen Ereignis in der Vergangenheit stattgefunden hat.

Bejahte und verneinte Formen des (*simple*) *past perfect*

Das (***simple***) ***past perfect*** ist für alle Personen gleich. Es wird aus ***had*** und dem ***past participle*** (siehe dazu Kapitel 3.1, Seite 34) gebildet.

I you he/she/it we you they	**had**	**(not)**	**played**

Die **Verneinung** bildest du, indem du ***not*** nach *had* einsetzt.

Du kannst in bejahten und verneinten Sätzen auch die entsprechenden **Kurzformen** verwenden:

He'**d** been there before. He **hadn't** seen her for years.

Entscheidungsfragen und Kurzantworten im (*simple*) *past perfect*

Für **Entscheidungsfragen** ziehst du ***had*** an den Satzanfang.
Auch die **Kurzantwort** bildest du mit ***had***:

Frage	Bejahte Kurzantwort	Verneinte Kurzantwort
Had he seen her?	Yes, **he had**.	No, **he hadn't**.

Ergänzungsfragen im (*simple*) *past perfect*

Bei Fragen nach dem Objekt/der adverbialen Bestimmung steht das Fragewort vor ***had*** am Anfang des Satzes (siehe Kapitel 1.1, Seite 9):

What	had	he	done?

Bei Fragen nach dem Subjekt bleibt die Satzstellung des Aussagesatzes erhalten (siehe Kapitel 1.1, Seite 9):

He	had	talked	to her.
Who	had	talked	to her?

Aufgabe 1: Preparing a barbecue

Mr Sportslover überraschte seine Familie gestern mit einer Grillparty. Was hatte er vorher alles vorbereitet? Setze die passenden Verben im (*simple*) *past perfect* in die Lücken ein.

hang up – surprise – prepare – invite – do – buy – carry

a) Mr Sportslover ______________________ his family with the idea of a barbecue (*Grillparty*).

b) He ______________________ some of their neighbors to their house.

c) He ______________________ all the necessary shopping.

d) He ______________________ some steaks in the supermarket.

e) He ______________________ the grill into the garden.

f) He ______________________ some colorful lanterns (*Laternen*) in the trees.

g) He ______________________ some ice cubes (*Eiswürfel*).

Aufgabe 2: What a mess!

Die Sportslovers konnten gestern nichts mehr finden, denn am Tag zuvor hatten sie alles an den falschen Platz geräumt ... Setze die Verben in Klammern in ihrer bejahten oder verneinten Form ins (*simple*) *past perfect*.

a) Emma ______________________________ (not put) the house keys into the hall.

b) She ______________________________ (put) them under her bed.

c) Jacob ______________________________ (not leave) his sunglasses on his desk.

d) He ______________________________ (leave) them on the washing machine.

e) Dad ______________________________ (not take) the phone to the living room.

f) He ______________________________ (take) it to the bathroom.

g) Jacob ______________________________ (not pack) his climbing equipment into his sports bag.

h) He ______________________________ (pack) it into an old suitcase.

i) Emma ______________________________ (not throw) her swimsuit into the laundry basket (*Wäschekorb*).

j) She ______________________________ (throw) her swimsuit into the garage.

k) Mom ______________________________ (not hide) her jewelry in the safe.

l) She ______________________________ (hide) it in a coffee cup.

Aufgabe 3: Do you know these people?

Setze die in Klammern angegebenen Verben in ihrer bejahten oder verneinten Form ins (*simple*) *past perfect*. Bilde Aussagesätze, Entscheidungsfragen oder Kurzantworten.

a) Marie Curie became famous because she ______________________ (discover) radioactivity (*Radioaktivität*).

b) ______________ she also ______________________ (discover) electricity? (*Elektrizität*) – No, she ______________________.

c) Did scientists talk about Konrad Zuse because he ______________________ (build) the first radio?

d) No, he ______________________ (not build) the first radio.

e) People admired him because he ______________________ (develop) one of the first computers in Germany.

f) Journalists wrote about Tim Berners-Lee because he ______________________ (invent – *erfinden, regelmäßiges Verb*) the World Wide Web.

e) ______________ he also ______________________ (invent) the telephone? No, he ______________________.

Aufgabe 4: The Internet

Frage jeweils nach dem unterstrichenen Satzteil.

a) <u>Nobody</u> had been able to imagine the great success of the Internet before it became popular in the 1990s.

b) Before 1969, scientists had tested a new communication system <u>for military (*militärisch*) reasons</u>.

c) The Internet had helped <u>the American military</u> to communicate secretly.

d) <u>The scientists</u> had spent many years of research on it.

e) <u>Their experiments</u> had failed (*misslingen*) many times before the scientists were finally successful.

4.2 Die Formen des *past perfect progressive*

Mit dem ***past perfect progressive*** drückst du aus, dass eine Handlung bis zu einem bestimmten Zeitpunkt in der Vergangenheit andauerte.

Bejahte und verneinte Formen des *past perfect progressive*

Das ***past perfect progressive*** ist für alle Personen gleich. Es wird aus ***had been*** und der ***ing*-Form** gebildet.

I you he/she/it we you they	**had**	**(not)**	***been***	***waiting***

Die **Verneinung** bildest du, indem du ***not*** nach ***had*** einsetzt.

Du kannst in bejahten und verneinten Sätzen auch die entsprechenden **Kurzformen** verwenden:
We**'d** been practicing since the early morning.
You **hadn't** been sleeping for more than a few minutes.

Entscheidungsfragen und Kurzantworten im *past perfect progressive*

Für **Entscheidungsfragen** ziehst du ***had*** an den Satzanfang. Auch die **Kurzantwort** bildest du mit ***had***:

Frage	Bejahte Kurzantwort	Verneinte Kurzantwort
Had he been working?	Yes, **he had**.	No, **he hadn't**.

Ergänzungsfragen im *past perfect progressive*

Bei Fragen nach dem Objekt/der adverbialen Bestimmung steht das Fragewort vor ***had*** am Anfang des Satzes (siehe Kapitel 1.1, Seite 9):

What	had	they	been	doing?

Bei Fragen nach dem Subjekt bleibt die Satzstellung des Aussagesatzes erhalten (siehe Kapitel 1.1, Seite 9):

Loud noises	had	been	scaring	them.
What	had	been	scaring	them?

Aufgabe 5: Before the casting show

Womit hatten die Kandidaten sich beschäftigt, bevor das Casting begann? Setze die in Klammern angegebenen Verben in ihrer bejahten oder verneinten Form ins *past perfect progressive*.

a) A tall boy ______________________________ (repeat) some dance steps over and over again.

b) Another boy ______________________________ (practice) his song for hours.

c) A girl ______________________________ (do) some breathing exercises.

d) Another girl ______________________________ (talk) to her boyfriend on the phone for ages.

e) A young man ______________________________ (brag – *prahlen*) about his success at an earlier casting.

f) A young woman ______________________________ (scare) the other candidates with stories about the strict judges (*Juroren*).

Aufgabe 6: Hard work

Schreibe auf, was alle diese Leute getan hatten bzw. nicht getan hatten, als endlich der Feierabend kam.

a) waiter: serve food to the customers/not wash plates

The waiter had been serving food to the customers.
He hadn't been washing plates.

b) surfing instructor: give lessons / not relax on the beach

____

____

c) janitor (*Hausmeister*): paint the walls / not repair the door

____

____

d) journalist: work on an article / not take pictures

____

____

e) tourist guide: talk about the sights / not sit in a café

____

____

f) student: do grammar exercises / not sleep

____

____

Aufgabe 7: What had they been doing?

Verwende noch einmal die Angaben aus Aufgabe 7. Bilde passende Entscheidungsfragen und Kurzantworten.

Beispiel: a) *Had the waiter been serving food to the customers?*
Yes, he had.
Had he been washing the plates? No, he hadn't.

Aufgabe 8: More about the casting show

Mrs Sportslover hat letzte Woche mit ihrer Freundin Betty bei einer Castingshow zugeschaut. Betty hat nicht alles mitbekommen und stellt ihr danach etliche Fragen. Bilde Aussagesätze und Fragen im *past perfect progressive* mithilfe der Angaben in Klammern.

a) Betty: "How long ______________________________

(the candidates – wait) before the show began?"

b) Mrs Sportslover: "______________________________

(they – wait) since early morning."

c) Betty: "What ______________________________

(they – show) when the audience clapped?"

d) Mrs Sportslover: "______________________________

(they – show) their talents (*Talente*)."

e) Betty: "Why ______________________________

(the judges – stare) at one of the candidates before they made their decision?"

f) Mrs Sportslover: "______________________________

(they – stare) at her because of her brilliant performance."

g) Betty: "How long ______________________________

(the judges – discuss) the candidates' performances until they decided on a winner?"

h) Mrs Sportslover: "______________________________

(they – discuss) for half an hour."

i) Betty: "Why ______________________________

(the winner of the show – cry) before the show ended?"

j) Mrs Sportslover: "______________________________

(she – cry) for joy."

4.3 Der Gebrauch von (*simple*) *past perfect* und *past perfect progressive*

Die Verwendung des (*simple*) *past perfect*

Mit dem **(*simple*) *past perfect*** drückst du aus, dass ein **Ereignis in der Vergangenheit** (Handlung 1) sich vor einem anderen **Ereignis in der Vergangenheit** (Handlung 2) ereignete und abgeschlossen war. Für die frühere Handlung verwendest du das (*simple*) *past perfect*, für die spätere Handlung meist das *simple past*.

After I **had eaten** lunch, I **did** my homework.
As soon as I **had arrived**, I **started** taking pictures.

Signalwörter: *after, when, as soon as*

Die Verwendung des *past perfect progressive*

Mit dem ***past perfect progressive*** betonst du, dass eine Handlung in der Vergangenheit (Handlung 1) bereits einige Zeit **angedauert hatte**, bevor eine andere Handlung (Handlung 2) begann. Für die frühere Handlung verwendest du das *past perfect progressive*, für die spätere Handlung das *simple past*.

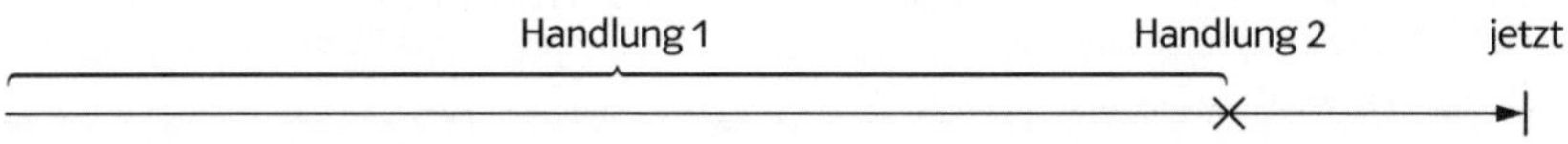

I had been standing there for hours when the bus arrived.

Signalwörter: *for, since, all/the whole morning/day/week/month*

Achtung:
Hilfsverben wie *can, must, to have got* bilden **keine Verlaufsform!**
Auch die Verben *to be, to like, to hate* und *to want* werden in der Regel nicht im *past perfect progressive* verwendet.

Aufgabe 9: Simple or progressive?

Suche die passenden Verben aus und setze sie im (*simple*) *past perfect* oder *past perfect progressive* in die Lücken ein.

walk – have – look for – try – ask – save – put on – think

a) Emma ______________________________ about her problem for days when she finally had an idea what to do about it.

b) The Sportslovers ______________________________ a lot of arguments about their vacation before they agreed on a compromise (*Kompromiss*).

c) Mom ______________________________ around in the rain for ten minutes until she found shelter (*Schutz*).

d) Dad ______________________________ the right present for Mom for weeks before he saw a suitable (*passend*) pair of earrings in a shop window.

e) Jacob ______________________________ to convince his parents of his opinion on tattoos time and again until he finally gave up.

f) Emma and Jacob ______________________________ their parents for more pocket money again and again until Mom and Dad agreed in the end.

g) After Lena's parents ______________________________ money for two years, they visited their relatives in the USA.

h) Jacob ______________________________ many different climbing shoes in the shop until he found the right ones.

Aufgabe 10: At the station

Eines der Verben musst du jeweils ins *simple past* setzen, das andere Verb ins (*simple*) *past perfect* oder *past perfect progressive*.

a) After the family ______________________ (wait) at the platform for half an hour, their train ______________________ (arrive).

b) The student ______________________ (buy) some chocolate before he ______________________ (go) to his train.

c) The businessman ______________________ (already – hear) the announcement about the delay of his train six times when he ______________________ (decide) to rent (*mieten*) a car.

d) The secretary ______________________ (look for) her husband in the station for quite some time when she finally ______________________ (discover) him in the book store.

e) The barman ______________________ (have) a little break after he ______________________ (make) many cups of coffee.

f) The couple ______________________ (take) a bus into the city center after they ______________________ (lock away) their bags.

g) The old man ______________________ (stand) in the line (*Schlange*) at the ticket office for twenty minutes when it ______________________ (be) finally his turn.

Abschlusstest online 4

Geschafft! Du hast das **Kapitel 4 – Das *past perfect*** durchgearbeitet. Hier ging es um die Zeit, die du im Englischen dazu benutzt, um etwas auszudrücken, das noch vor einem anderen vergangenen Ereignis passierte. Auch diese Zeit gibt es wieder in zwei Formen: als *simple past perfect* für den Normalfall und als *past perfect progressive* für Handlungen, die zu einem bestimmten Zeitpunkt noch andauerten.

So funktioniert der Abschlusstest online:
Um deinen Lernerfolg zu überprüfen, kannst du nun die Abschlusstests machen. Gehe auf
https://www.klett-lerntraining.de/5N5D
und wähle das Kapitel und einen Test aus.

Welche Tests es gibt, siehst du unten in der Tabelle. Nach jedem Test bekommst du eine Auswertung.

Willst du immer im Blick haben, welche Themen du schon kannst oder was du besser wiederholen solltest? Dann schreibe deine Ergebnisse in die Tabelle.

Mein Ergebnis im Abschlusstest online – Kapitel 4

Thema	Mein Ergebnis
Die Formen des (*simple*) *past perfect*	
Die Formen des *past perfect progressive*	
Der Gebrauch von (*simple*) *past perfect* und *past perfect progressive*	

5 Die Zeitformen der Zukunft

5.1 Die Formen des *will-future*

Mit dem ***will-future*** kannst du über Zukünftiges sprechen. Du musst es verwenden, wenn du Vermutungen über die Zukunft äußern willst oder über zukünftige Ereignisse sprichst, die du nicht beeinflussen kannst.

Bejahte und verneinte Form des *will-future*

Das *will-future* wird gebildet aus ***will*** **+ Infinitiv des Verbs**. Das *will-future* lautet für alle Personen gleich.

I you he/she/it we you they	**will**	**(not)**	**come**

Zur Verneinung setzt du ***not*** nach ***will*** ein.

Du kannst in bejahten und verneinten Sätzen auch die entsprechenden **Kurzformen** verwenden:
She'**ll** answer your letter. He **won't** write back to you.

Entscheidungsfragen und Kurzantworten im *will-future*

Für **Entscheidungsfragen** ziehst du ***will*** an den Satzanfang. Auch die **Kurzantwort** bildest du mit ***will***:

Frage	Bejahte Kurzantwort	Verneinte Kurzantwort
Will you come?	Yes, **I will.**	No, **I won't**.

Ergänzungsfragen im *will-future*

Bei Fragen nach dem Objekt/der adverbialen Bestimmung steht das Fragewort vor ***will*** am Anfang des Satzes (siehe Kapitel 1.1, Seite 9):

When	will	he	be back?

Bei Fragen nach dem Subjekt bleibt die Satzstellung des Aussagesatzes erhalten (siehe Kapitel 1.1, Seite 9):

Jacob	will	come	to our party.
Who	will	come	to our party?

Aufgabe 1: A weather forecast (Wettervorhersage)

Setze die in Klammern angegebenen Verben in die bejahte oder verneinte Form des *will-future*.

a) There ______________________________ (be) lots of sunshine today.

b) You ______________________________ (need) a sun hat and sunglasses.

c) You ______________________________ (not see) a cloud in the sky.

d) A very warm night ______________________________ (make) it difficult to get some sleep.

e) But it ______________________________ (give) you the chance of having a nice barbecue with your family and friends.

f) It ______________________________ (not rain) until the morning.

g) Heavy thunderstorms ______________________________ (bring) a change of weather tomorrow.

h) For the rest of the week, the temperatures ______________________________ (not rise) as high as before.

Aufgabe 2: Your opinion about sports

Bilde mithilfe der vorgegebenen Stichpunkte Entscheidungsfragen und schreibe sie auf. Das Verb setzt du ins *will-future*. Antworte in Form einer Kurzantwort mit Ja oder Nein, je nachdem, welche Meinung du vertrittst.

a) the German team – be – next soccer world champion

Will the German team be the next soccer world champion?
Yes, it will./No, it won't.

b) racing cars – soon – go – faster than 500 km/h

c) handball – become – more popular than soccer

d) German schools – offer – their students – skateboarding instead of normal sports classes

e) Olympic Games – still – exist – in fifty years

f) German soccer players – play – like Brazilians – one day

Aufgabe 3: America's future

Schreibe die Fragen in der richtigen Reihenfolge auf. Setze das Verb in Klammern ins *will-future*.

a) the next President of the USA – who – (be)

b) American scientists – (invent) – when – the next big thing

c) (win) – who – the next film award (*Filmpreis*)

d) the next snowstorm – when – (hit) – California

e) how many people – in the USA – (live) – in twenty years

f) the title (*Titel*) of the next number one song – (be) – what

Aufgabe 4: The fortune teller (Wahrsagerin)

Emma hat heute zum Spaß eine Wahrsagerin am berühmten Venice Beach in Los Angeles besucht. Ob alles, was sie erfährt, der Wahrheit entspricht? Ergänze die Aussagesätze und Fragen im *will-future*.

a) Emma: "______________________________ (you – tell) me something about my future?"

b) Fortune teller: "______________________________ (I – inform) you about everything you need to know. Just ask your questions."

c) Emma: "______________________________ (five dollars – be) enough for your answers?"

d) Fortune teller: "Pay me later. I am sure that ______________________________ (my answers – be) worth a lot to you."

e) Emma: "Okay. What ______________________________ (I – do) when I have finished school?"

f) Fortune teller: "______________________________ (you – become) a famous movie star."

g) Emma: "Where ______________________________ (I – live)?"

h) Fortune teller: "______________________________ (you – own) houses in New York, London and Berlin."

i) Emma: "______________________________ (I – have) children?"

j) Fortune teller: "______________________________ (you – be) the mother of seven great children."

k) Emma: "______________________________ (I – be) married?"

l) Fortune teller: "______________________________ (you – get) married five times."

5.2 Die Formen des *going to-future*

Um einen Plan oder eine feste Absicht für die nahe Zukunft zu beschreiben, kannst du das ***going to-future*** verwenden.

Bejahte und verneinte Form des *going to-future*

Du bildest das *going to-future* aus ***am/is/are* + *going to* + Infinitiv**:

I you he/she/it we you they	**am** **are** **is** **are** **are** **are**	**(not)**	**going to**	**visit.**

Zur Verneinung setzt du ***not*** nach ***am/is/are*** ein.

Du kannst in bejahten und verneinten Sätzen auch die entsprechenden **Kurzformen** verwenden:

I**'m** going to watch a soccer match.
He**'s** going to play basketball.

I**'m not** going to watch a movie.
He **isn't** going to play soccer.

Entscheidungsfragen und Kurzantworten im *going to-future*

Zur Bildung von **Entscheidungsfragen** ziehst du die Form von ***to be*** an den Satzanfang. Eine Form von ***to be*** verwendest du auch in der **Kurzantwort**.

Frage	Bejahte Kurzantwort	Verneinte Kurzantwort
Is he going to help?	Yes, **he is**.	No, **he isn't**.

Ergänzungsfragen im *going to-future*

Bei Fragen nach dem Objekt oder der adverbialen Bestimmung (siehe Kapitel 1.1, Seite 9) ziehst du das Fragewort vor die Form von ***to be*** an den Satzanfang.

Where	is	she	going to	go?

Bei Fragen nach dem Subjekt (siehe Kapitel 1.1, Seite 9) bleibt die Satzstellung des Aussagesatzes erhalten.

Emma	is	going to	do	this exercise.
Who	is	going to	do	this exercise?

Aufgabe 5: A trip to Europe

Finde die in der Wörterschlange versteckten Verben. Sie stehen bereits in der richtigen Reihenfolge. Setze sie im *going to-future* in die Lücken ein.

visitzuzspendvenhaveuipbuyxyxflyrtzlistenmonseesiotake

a) The American tourists ______________________________ Germany first.

b) They ______________________________ three days in Berlin.

c) They ______________________________ a look at some popular sights, like the Brandenburg Gate (*Brandenburger Tor*).

d) They ______________________________ a piece of stone from the Berlin Wall.

e) Later they ______________________________ from Berlin to Munich.

f) They ______________________________ to traditional (*traditionelle*) bands at the Oktoberfest.

g) Finally they ______________________________ Hamburg.

h) They ______________________________ a look at the harbor there.

Aufgabe 6: What are they going to change?

Hier geht es um Vorsätze für das neue Jahr. Suche passende Verben aus und setze sie im *going to-future* in die Lücken ein.

eat – not drink – work – do – not spend –
learn – not watch – go – not get up – stop

a) He ______________________________ smoking.

b) They ______________________________ more fruit and vegetables.

c) She ______________________________ harder at school.

d) I ______________________________ as much TV anymore.

e) You ______________________________ sports three times a week.

f) He ______________________________ to work by bike.

g) They ______________________________ beer (*Bier*) anymore.

h) She ______________________________ new languages.

i) He ______________________________ so late in the mornings anymore.

j) I ______________________________ so much money on clothes anymore.

Aufgabe 7: Parents' questions

Schreibe die Fragen in der richtigen Reihenfolge auf. Setze dabei das Verb in Klammern jeweils ins *going to-future*.

a) (do) – when – your homework – you

b) (meet) – who – you – tonight

c) where – next – you – (go)

d) your room – you – (clean up) – when

e) (do) – about your grades (*Noten*) – what – you

Aufgabe 8: What now?

Bilde Aussagesätze, Fragen und Kurzantworten im *going to-future* mithilfe der Angaben in Klammern.

a) The Sportslovers' car has broken down.

What ____ (they – do) now?

b) ____ (they – buy) a new car? – No, ____.

c) ____ (Dad – repair: *reparieren*) the old one.

d) Mom has lost the recipe for Emma's favorite cake.

Where ____ (she – look for) it?

e) ____ (she – search for) a similar (*ähnlich*) recipe on the Internet.

f) Then ____ (she – bake) Emma's birthday cake.

g) Jacob has left the shopping list at home.

____ (he – go) back home and get it? – No, ____.

h) ____ (he – call) his parents on his cell phone (*Handy*) …

i) … and then ____ (he – ask) them what to buy at the supermarket.

5.3 Der Gebrauch von *will-future, going to-future, simple present* und *present progressive*

Im Englischen hast du, anders als im Deutschen, viele verschiedene Möglichkeiten, Zukünftiges auszudrücken, je nachdem wie sicher ein bestimmtes Ereignis ist und wie stark du es selbst beeinflussen kannst.

In diesen Fällen verwendest du das *going to-future*:

- Wenn du einen Plan oder eine bestimmte Absicht hast:
  She**'s going to run** a marathon tomorrow.
- Wenn du über absehbare Ereignisse der nahen Zukunft sprichst, für die es bereits Anzeichen gibt:
  Look at the player's angry face! He**'s going to start** an argument with the referee any minute.
  → Der ärgerliche Gesichtsausdruck des Spielers zeigt bereits an, dass er gleich einen Streit anfängt.

In diesen Fällen verwendest du das *will-future*:

- Wenn du über Ereignisse in der Zukunft sprichst, die du nicht selbst beeinflussen kannst, sondern die von äußeren Umständen abhängen:
  Will he **win** the lottery (*im Lotto*)?
- Wenn du Vermutungen über die Zukunft ausdrückst:
  I think the English football team **will lose**.
  Signalwörter: *I think, I promise, I hope, I'm sure, probably*
- Wenn du eine spontane Entscheidung triffst:
  Can anyone close the door, please? – Okay, I**'ll do** it.

In diesen Fällen verwendest du das *simple present* für Zukünftiges:

- Wenn du über feste, oft sogar regelmäßige Termine in der Zukunft sprichst, besonders bei Programmen (z. B. Fernsehen, Kino, Theater, Sportveranstaltungen) und Fahrplänen. Deshalb bezeichnet man es auch als *timetable future*. In der Regel gibst du eine genaue Uhrzeit bzw. ein genaues Datum mit an:
  The film **starts** at 8.30 pm.
  The train **leaves** at 11 o'clock.
  The festival **ends** on Wednesday, August 31st.

In diesen Fällen verwendest du das *present progressive* für Zukünftiges:

- Wenn du über Pläne sprichst, die fest ausgemacht sind. Weil sie oft in den Kalender eingetragen werden, bezeichnet man es auch als *diary future*. Damit man gleich erkennt, dass es um die Zukunft geht, stehen meist Zeitangaben wie *this afternoon, tomorrow, next week* mit im Satz:
  Tonight I **am having** dinner with my parents at an Italian restaurant.
  I **am meeting** Jo at the youth club tomorrow.

Unterschied zur deutschen Zeitenverwendung:

- Das deutsche **Präsens** musst du im Englischen oft mit dem ***going to-future*** oder ***will-future*** übersetzen:
  Sie **nimmt** nächsten Monat Fahrstunden.
  She**'s going to take** driving lessons next month.
  Morgen **ist** sicher viel Verkehr.
  I'm sure there **will be** lots of traffic tomorrow.
- Denke daran, dass die Formen des ***present tense*** im Englischen nur in ganz bestimmten Fällen zum Ausdruck von Zukünftigem verwendet werden!

Aufgabe 9: Using different future forms

Suche jeweils die passende Verbform heraus.

will start – are going to start – starts

a) The soccer game ______________________ at 3 pm today.

b) The players ______________________ their warm-up exercises soon.

c) I think the coach ______________________ giving his last instructions (*Anweisungen*) right before the game in a couple of minutes.

will open – won't open – is going to open

d) Jacob ______________________ the fridge because he is very hungry.

e) What bad luck! It is empty. And the new supermarket down the road ______________________ until next year.

f) But his mother tells him: "Don't worry, Jacob. I ______________________ a can (*Dose*) of soup for you."

will go – are going – are going to go

g) Emma and Jacob ______________________ to a beach party tonight.

h) They are wearing their swimsuits. ______________________ they ______________________ swimming?

i) Everybody is having a lot of fun at the beach. I think Emma and Jacob ______________________ home very late today.

Aufgabe 10: A flight into space (*Weltraum*)

Welche Verbform passt in die Lücke? Kreuze die richtige Lösung an.

a) The astronauts (*Astronauten*) ______ an interview to a TV station before the flight this afternoon.

☐ are giving ☐ give

b) The astronauts aren't sure whether the rocket (*Rakete*) ______ on time.

☐ is taking off ☐ will take off

c) Luckily, it is a good day for this space project. There aren't any clouds in the sky. The sun ______ all afternoon.

☐ is going to shine ☐ will shine

d) It is certain that there ______ any weather problems for the astronauts.

☐ aren't ☐ won't be

e) The mechanics (*Mechaniker*) are walking to the rocket now. They ______ all the instruments on board.

☐ check ☐ are going to check

f) The astronauts ______ good-bye to their families soon.

☐ are going to say ☐ say

g) The scientists are very excited. They hope that this project ______ a success.

☐ will be ☐ is going to be

h) Hurry! Come in and sit down. The TV program about the astronauts ______ in a few minutes.

☐ is going to start ☐ starts

Aufgabe 11: Travel plans

In dieser Übung geht es um die Reisepläne von Lena und ihrer Familie. Sie wollen auf ihrer Rückreise einen Zwischenstopp in New York einlegen. Nur eine der beiden angegebenen Verbformen ist jeweils richtig. Streiche die falsche Verbform durch.

a) Mrs Sportslover drives / is driving Lena and her family to the airport in Los Angeles next Friday.

b) The plane to New York leaves / will leave in the early morning.

c) The flight will last / is lasting about six hours.

d) Lena is going to read / will read an English book by her favorite author during the flight.

e) The plane lands / is going to land at John F. Kennedy airport in New York at 3 pm.

f) Lena and her family are taking / are going to take a cab from the airport in New York to their hotel.

g) They hope that their hotel room won't be / isn't going to be too small.

h) But probably they aren't spending / won't spend a lot of time there anyway.

i) They are going to do / will do a lot of sightseeing in New York.

j) They have already booked tickets for a musical on Broadway. The show is / will be on Sunday night.

k) Lena promises her cousins that she is going to call / will call them from New York.

l) She hopes they are visiting / will visit her in Germany next year.

Abschlusstest online 5

Wow, gut gemacht! Du hast das **Kapitel 5 – Die Zeitformen der Zukunft** durchgearbeitet, und da gibt es im Englischen ja einige! Nicht nur *will-future* und *going to-future*, sondern sogar die Gegenwartszeiten *simple present* und *present progressive* können in bestimmten Fällen benutzt werden, um Zukünftiges auszudrücken.

So funktioniert der Abschlusstest online:
Um deinen Lernerfolg zu überprüfen, kannst du nun die Abschlusstests machen. Gehe auf
https://www.klett-lerntraining.de/5N5D
und wähle das Kapitel und einen Test aus.

Welche Tests es gibt, siehst du unten in der Tabelle. Nach jedem Test bekommst du eine Auswertung.

Willst du immer im Blick haben, welche Themen du schon kannst oder was du besser wiederholen solltest? Dann schreibe deine Ergebnisse in die Tabelle.

Mein Ergebnis im Abschlusstest online – Kapitel 5

Thema	Mein Ergebnis
Die Formen des *will-future*	
Die Formen des *going to-future*	
Der Gebrauch von *will-future*, *going to-future*, *simple present* und *present progressive*	

6 Modalverben und ihre Ersatzformen

6.1 Die Ersatzformen *be able to, be allowed to* und *have to*

Können: *can* und *be able to*

Das Modalverb ***can*** drückt unter anderem aus, dass du etwas tun **kannst**, das heißt, dass du fähig und in der Lage bist, etwas zu tun. Die verneinte Form lautet ***cannot*** oder ***can't***.

Als einziges Modalverb kann ***can*** ins ***simple past*** gesetzt werden. Die bejahte Form lautet ***could***, die verneinte ***could not*** bzw. ***couldn't***.

Alle anderen Zeiten müssen mithilfe der Ersatzform **(*not*) *be able to*** gebildet werden. Du kannst diese Ersatzform aber auch im *present tense* und *simple past* verwenden.

Dürfen: *can, may, mustn't* und *be allowed to*

Mit ***can*** kannst du auch ausdrücken, dass du etwas tun **darfst**. Die gleiche Bedeutung hat das Modalverb ***may***. Die verneinte Form von ***may*** lautet ***may not***.

Die verneinte Form ***must not*/*mustn't*** drückt aus, dass du etwas **nicht** tun **darfst**.

Die Modalverben ***may***, ***must*** und ***mustn't*** kannst du **nur** im ***simple present*** verwenden. Alle anderen Zeiten müssen mithilfe der Ersatzform **(*not*) *be allowed to*** gebildet werden. Du kannst diese Ersatzform aber auch im *present tense* und *simple past* verwenden.

Müssen: *must, needn't* und *have to*

Mit ***must*** drückst du aus, dass du etwas tun **musst**. Als Verneinung von ***must*** wird ***need not*/*needn't*** (etwas nicht zu tun brauchen) verwendet. Beide Verben können nur im *simple present* verwendet werden. Alle anderen Zeiten müssen mithilfe der Ersatzform **(*not*) *have to*** gebildet werden. Du kannst diese Ersatzform aber auch im *present tense* verwenden.

Die Modalverben und ihre Ersatzformen im Überblick

	können	**dürfen**	**müssen**
simple present	can	can/may mustn't	must needn't
	am/is/are (not) able to	am/is/are (not) allowed to	have/has to do not/does not have to
simple past	could	could	
	was/were (not) able to	was/were (not) allowed to	had to did not have to
(*simple*) *present perfect*	have/has (not) been able to	have/has (not) been allowed to	have/has (not) had to
(*simple*) *past perfect*	had (not) been able to	had (not) been allowed to	had (not) had to
will-future	will (not) be able to	will (not) be allowed to	will (not) have to

Aufgabe 1: Rules in the Rocky Mountains

In den Rocky Mountains gibt es viele Warnhinweise für Touristen. Formuliere diese Warnhinweise mithilfe der Modalverben im *simple present* um.

Beispiel: a) *Tourists must not climb this mountain in the event of a thunderstorm.*

a)

Do not climb this mountain in the event of a thunderstorm.

b)

Always stay on the trails.

c)

Do not feed bears or other wild animals.

d)

Do not use bicycles on the trails.

e)

Keep away from the icy river.

f)

Fishing allowed here only with a fishing license.

b) trail: *Wanderweg* f) license: *Erlaubnis*

Aufgabe 2: Talking about rules in the Rockies

Ersetze die Modalverben aus Aufgabe 1 durch ihre Ersatzformen. Schreibe ganze Sätze auf.

Beispiel: a) *Tourists aren't allowed to climb this mountain in the event of a thunderstorm.*

Aufgabe 3: At the training camp

Setze die passenden Modalverben oder ihre Ersatzformen im *simple present* ein.

a) Jacob and some of his friends got places at a training camp for young climbers. They ______________________ (*können*) go there later this summer.

b) They ______________________ (*dürfen*) stay there for a couple of days.

c) They ______________________ (*nicht müssen*) take their parents with them.

d) At the camp they ______________________ (*müssen*) get up very early.

e) The climbers there ______________________ (*können*) teach each other different climbing techniques (*Klettertechniken*).

f) The most important rule is that they ______________________ (*nicht dürfen*) climb alone.

g) The teenagers at the camp ______________________ (*nicht können*) hang out much …

h) … because they ______________________ (*müssen*) do a lot of sports.

i) There is no electricity at the camp, so the young climbers ______________________ (*nicht können*) watch TV in the evenings.

j) But at least they ______________________ (*nicht müssen*) do schoolwork while they are at the camp.

Aufgabe 4: Talking about the training camp again

Setze die Sätze aus Aufgabe 3 unter Verwendung passender Ersatzformen der Modalverben ins *simple past*.

Beispiel: a) Jacob and some of his friends were able to get places at a training camp for young climbers.

Aufgabe 5: Rules for young people in Germany

Setze die Ersatzformen der Modalverben in die passende Zeit (*simple present, simple past, present perfect* oder *will-future*). In Klammern ist jeweils die deutsche Bedeutung der gesuchten Ersatzform angegeben.

a) Since 2007 teenagers under 18 ______________________________ ______________________________ (*nicht dürfen*) smoke in public.

b) Since 2009 underage (*minderjährig*) young people ______________________________ ______________________________ (*nicht können*) buy cigarettes from vending machines (*Zigarettenautomat*).

c) But in 2008 everybody ______________________________ ______________________________ (*können*) use cigarette vending machines.

d) Since 2011 young people in Germany ______________________________ ______________________________ (*dürfen*) get their driver's license at the age of 17.

e) But in 2008 they usually ______________________________ ______________________________ (*müssen*) wait until they were 18.

f) Some teenagers hope that they ______________________________ soon ______________________________ (*dürfen*) vote at the age of 16.

g) At the moment, everybody who is at least 18 ______________________________ ______________________________ (*dürfen*) vote.

h) Until 1970 you ______________________________ ______________________________ (*nicht dürfen*) vote for (*wählen*) the members of parliament (*Abgeordneten*) if you were under 21.

i) For many years now teenagers under 16 ______________________________ ______________________________ (*müssen*) be with their parents to go to dance clubs.

Aufgabe 6: Women's soccer

Setze die in Klammern angegebenen Ersatzformen der Modalverben in die richtige Zeit: *simple past, present perfect* oder *past perfect*?

a) In 1970, women ______________________________ ______ (*be allowed to*) play in public stadiums (*Stadions*) for the first time.

b) Before that female (*weibliche*) soccer teams ______________________________ ______________________________ (*not be allowed to*) use them.

c) The countries of the world ______________________________ ______________________________ (*be able to*) send their female soccer teams to a world cup as late as 1991.

d) Before that the German team ______________________________ ______________________________ (*be able to*) play in European competitions for several years.

e) Since 1993 women's soccer games ______________________________ ______________________________ (*be allowed to*) last for 90 minutes.

f) Before the DFB decided on this change, the two halves of a game ______ ______________________________ (*have to*) finish after 40 minutes each.

g) In 2007 the German team ______________________________ ______________________________ (*be able to*) win the world cup for the second time.

h) The German players ______________________________ already ______________ ______________________________ (*be able to*) win this competition in 2003.

i) But they ______________________________ (*not be able to*) repeat this success in 2011.

j) Because of that, they ______________________________ (*have to*) live with a lot of negative press coverage (*negative Presse*).

6.2 Modalverben mit dem Infinitiv Perfekt

Die Modalverben ***must***, ***could***, ***might***, ***should*** und ***needn't*** können auch mit dem **Infinitiv Perfekt** (*perfect infinitive*) verwendet werden, also mit ***have*** **+ Partizip Perfekt**.

	Modalverb	Infinitiv Perfekt		deutsche Entsprechung
You	**must**	**have seen**	her.	*musst … gesehen haben*
He	**could**	**have done**	more.	*hätte … tun können*
She	**might**	**have heard**	it.	*hat vielleicht … gehört*
We	**should**	**have written**	a card.	*hätten … schreiben sollen*
They	**needn't**	**have listened.**		*hätten nicht zuhören müssen*

Mit dieser Konstruktion beziehst du dich auf die Vergangenheit:
Es geht um Ereignisse, die passiert sein mussten oder hätten geschehen müssen, können oder sollen. Du kannst auch ausdrücken, dass etwas wahrscheinlich oder vielleicht passiert ist.

Aufgabe 7: What might have been

Bilde Sätze mit Modalverben und dem Infinitiv Perfekt. Bringe dazu die vorgegebenen Satzteile in die richtige Reihenfolge und setze die Verben in Klammern in den Infinitiv Perfekt.

a) (hear of) – you – must – that new TV show

b) that horror movie – I – shouldn't – (watch)

c) the live concert – he – needn't – (record: *aufnehmen*; *regelmäßiges Verb*)

d) (laugh) – we – might – about that comedian

e) (imagine) – they – couldn't – a more exciting thriller

Aufgabe 8: Sports, sports, sports

Bilde mithilfe der in den Bildern dargestellten Situationen und der angegebenen Verben Sätze mit Modalverben und dem Infinitiv Perfekt.

Beispiel: a) *The tennis player must have lost the match.*

tennis player / lose the match

goalie (*Torwart*) / stop the ball

cyclist / exercise (*trainieren*) more

referee / make an unfair decision

basketball player / jump higher

swimmer / worry about the competition

mountain biker / wear a helmet

runner / think of wearing running shoes

surfer / put on sunscreen (*Sonnencreme*)

Aufgabe 9: At the hostel

Ergänze die zu den beschriebenen Situationen passenden Modalverben und setze die in Klammern angegebenen Verben in den Infinitiv Perfekt.

a) A guest's jacket has disappeared from his room.
   Somebody *must have stolen* (steal) it.

b) A boy broke a few cups in the kitchen.
   He ______________________________ (be) more careful.

c) The staff at the hostel (*Herbergspersonal*) prepared too many steaks for the barbecue. They ______________________________ (buy) so much meat.

d) A girl lost the key to her room.
   She ______________________________ (look) after her things better.

e) Breakfast is included (*inbegriffen*) in the price of a room. The young man ______________________________ (take) his own food with him.

f) One of the students arrived after the hostel curfew (*Schließstunde*).
   He ______________________________ (come) earlier.

g) A young woman found a ring in the bathroom.
   Somebody ______________________________ (leave) it there.

h) The staff at the hostel put too many guests into one room.
   They ______________________________ (check) the number of beds more carefully.

Abschlusstest online 6

Glückwunsch! Du hast das **Kapitel 6 – Modalverben und ihre Ersatzformen** durchgearbeitet. Jetzt bist du bestens im Bilde über alle Möglichkeiten, die du im Englischen hast, um Können, Müssen und Dürfen auszudrücken.

So funktioniert der Abschlusstest online:
Um deinen Lernerfolg zu überprüfen, kannst du nun die Abschlusstests machen. Gehe auf
https://www.klett-lerntraining.de/5N5D
und wähle das Kapitel und einen Test aus.

Welche Tests es gibt, siehst du unten in der Tabelle. Nach jedem Test bekommst du eine Auswertung.

Willst du immer im Blick haben, welche Themen du schon kannst oder was du besser wiederholen solltest? Dann schreibe deine Ergebnisse in die Tabelle.

Mein Ergebnis im Abschlusstest online – Kapitel 6

Thema	Mein Ergebnis
Die Ersatzformen *be able to*, *be allowed to* und *have to*	
Modalverben mit dem Infinitiv Perfekt	

7 Das *gerund*

7.1 Das *gerund* als Subjekt oder Objekt

Das ***gerund*** wird gebildet aus **dem Infinitiv** des Vollverbs und der Endung ***ing*** (z. B. *playing, reading*), es handelt sich also um eine *ing*-Form. Die Regeln für die Schreibung der *ing*-Form kannst du in Kapitel 1.2 (Seite 12) nachlesen.

Das *gerund* als Subjekt des Satzes

Das *gerund* kannst du genau wie ein Nomen als **Subjekt** des Satzes verwenden. Es kann auch zusammen mit anderen Wörtern das Subjekt bilden:

Subjekt	
Cycling **Playing** soccer **Being** nasty	is good for your health. is his favorite hobby. isn't a good idea.

Das *gerund* als Objekt des Satzes

Du kannst das *gerund* (ebenfalls mit anderen Wörtern zusammen) auch als **Objekt** des Satzes verwenden.

	Objekt
Many young people from California enjoy They like They imagined	**surfing**. **playing** beach volleyball. **winning** the match.

Besonders oft steht das *gerund* nach Verben, die ausdrücken, dass man etwas mag oder nicht mag:
to enjoy, to hate, to like, to love, to mind, to prefer, can't stand
Achtung: *would like to* **muss** immer mit dem **Infinitiv** stehen!

Außerdem steht nach folgenden Verben das *gerund*:
to finish, to start, to begin, to stop, to imagine, to keep, to miss, to risk

Aufgabe 1: Your hobbies and interests

Bilde zehn Sätze über deine Hobbies und Vorlieben mithilfe der vorgegebenen Bausteine. Die Verben im ersten Kasten musst du ins *gerund* setzen.

a) bowl with my friends b) surf the Internet c) talk on the phone d) play soccer e) solve puzzles f) listen to music g) act in a drama group h) look after my pet i) read books j) collect model cars	is isn't	my favorite hobby. something I like very much. an exciting activity. a good idea. a lot of fun.

Aufgabe 2: Parents' advice

Hier sind einige Ratschläge und Verhaltensregeln für Jugendliche, wie du sie vielleicht auch schon von deinen Eltern bekommen hast. Setze die Verben in der Form des *gerund* in die jeweils passende Lücke ein.

chat – stay – play – smoke – drink

a) ______________________ with strangers on the Internet can be dangerous.

b) ______________________ alcopops is bad for your health.

c) ______________________ up all night isn't good for you.

d) ______________________ computer games for hours is something you shouldn't do.

e) ______________________ cigarettes is a very bad idea.

7.2 Das *gerund* nach Präpositionen

Das *gerund* nach Verb + Präposition

Du benutzt das *gerund* nach bestimmten Verbindungen aus Verb und Präposition. Dazu gehören:
to feel like, to keep on, to look forward to, to worry about, to care about

	Verb + Präposition	***gerund***		**deutsche Entsprechung**
He	worries about	**losing**	his job.	... *hat Angst,* ... *zu verlieren*
We	are looking forward to	**meeting**	our friends.	... *freuen uns darauf,* ... *zu sehen*
I	feel like	**eating**	some ice-cream.	... *habe Lust darauf,* ... *zu essen*

Im Deutschen werden die verschiedenen Konstruktionen mit Präposition und *gerund* meist mit dem Infinitiv + zu wiedergegeben.

Das *gerund* nach Adjektiv + Präposition

Das *gerund* verwendest du auch nach bestimmten Verbindungen aus Adjektiv und Präposition, wie z. B.:
to be bad/good at, to be crazy about, to be interested in, to be tired of, to be used to

	Adjektiv + Präposition	***gerund***		**deutsche Entsprechung**
You are	good at	**playing**	badminton.	... *kannst gut* ... *spielen*
She is	used to	**practicing**	every day.	... *ist daran gewöhnt,* ... *zu üben*
I am	tired of	**hearing**	your excuses.	... *habe es satt,* ... *zu hören*

Das *gerund* nach Nomen + Präposition

Das *gerund* gebrauchst du ebenfalls nach vielen Verbindungen aus **Nomen + Präposition**. Dazu gehören z. B.:
a chance of, in danger of, the idea of, the risk of

	Nomen + Präposition	***gerund***		**deutsche Entsprechung**
There is always	a chance of	**winning.**		*… die Chance, zu gewinnen*
He is in	danger of	**falling**	off the bike.	*… in Gefahr, … zu fallen*
She likes	the idea of	**meeting**	people from all over the world.	*… die Idee, … zu treffen*

Aufgabe 3: Grammar exercises

Setze das in Klammern angegebene Verb in die Form des *gerund* und wähle aus den angegebenen Präpositionen die passende aus.

of – on – to – about – of – like – on

a) Are you looking forward ______________ ______________________ (finish) this exercise?

b) Do you feel ______________ ______________________ (close) this book?

c) Are you getting tired ______________ ______________________ (study) grammar?

d) Do you dream ______________ ______________________ (do) something else?

e) Don't worry ______________ ______________________ (spend) too much time on English grammar.

f) Keep ______________ ______________________ (improve) your English.

Aufgabe 4: Emma's and Jacob's dreams

Finde aus den angegebenen Adjektiven und Nomen jeweils das zu der Präposition passende heraus. Setze außerdem die in Klammern angegebenen Verben in die Form des *gerund*.

tired – interested – idea – good

a) Emma has the ____________________ of ____________________ (travel) across Europe one day.

b) She is ____________________ in ____________________ (learn) about other cultures.

c) She never gets ____________________ of ____________________ (experience) new things.

d) She is ____________________ at ____________________ (make) friends.

used – crazy – afraid – chance

e) Jacob has the ____________________ of ____________________ (become) a professional athlete (*Sportler*) one day.

f) He is ____________________ about ____________________ (do) his exercises three times a day.

g) He is ____________________ of ____________________ (have) to sit in an office all day in the future.

h) He doesn't get tired easily because he is ____________________ to ____________________ (work out: *trainieren*) a few times a week.

7.3 Der Gebrauch von Infinitiv und *gerund* nach bestimmten Verben

Gleiche Bedeutung von Infinitiv und *gerund*

Einige Verben kannst du sowohl mit Infinitiv als auch mit *gerund* verwenden, ohne dass sich die Bedeutung ändert, wie z. B.:
to like, to begin, to start, to love, to hate, to prefer
You **like dancing**. You **like to dance**.

Bedeutungsunterschied zwischen Infinitiv und *gerund*

Es gibt jedoch auch Verben, die in Kombination mit dem Infinitiv etwas anderes bedeuten als mit dem *gerund*:

	gerund	**Infinitiv**
to stop	**to stop doing** sth *aufhören, etwas zu tun / eine Handlung abbrechen*	**to stop to do** sth *anhalten/stehen bleiben, um etwas anderes/Neues zu tun*
to go on	**to go on doing** sth *mit etwas weitermachen / eine Handlung fortführen*	**to go on to do** sth *weitermachen, aber mit etwas anderem/Neuem*
to forget	**to forget doing** sth *vergessen, dass man etwas getan hat*	**to forget to do** sth *vergessen, etwas zu tun*
to remember	**to remember doing** sth *sich an etwas erinnern, das man getan hat*	**to remember to do** sth *daran denken, etwas (das noch bevorsteht) zu tun*
to mean	**to mean doing** sth *etwas bedeuten*	**to mean to do** sth *beabsichtigen, etwas zu tun*
to try	**to try doing** sth *einen bestimmten Weg / eine Methode ausprobieren; es mit etwas versuchen*	**to try to do** sth *versuchen, etwas Bestimmtes zu tun (es ist nicht klar, ob man es schafft)*

Aufgabe 5: Home schooling

Setze die in Klammern angegebenen Verben in die Form des *gerund*. Entscheide anschließend, ob jeweils auch der Infinitiv ohne Bedeutungsänderung möglich wäre.

a) Can you imagine ______________________ (go) to school in your own house or apartment?

Infinitiv: ☐ möglich ☐ nicht möglich

b) Some American parents don't like ______________________ (send) their children to public schools.

Infinitiv: ☐ möglich ☐ nicht möglich

c) They prefer ______________________ (teach) their children themselves.

Infinitiv: ☐ möglich ☐ nicht möglich

d) Sometimes a child starts ______________________ (take) lessons at home because of a long illness (*Krankheit*).

Infinitiv: ☐ möglich ☐ nicht möglich

e) Teenage actors will often risk ______________________ (miss) too many lessons if they go to a normal school.

Infinitiv: ☐ möglich ☐ nicht möglich

f) Private lessons enable (*ermöglichen*) them to keep ______________________ (study) even when shooting a film.

Infinitiv: ☐ möglich ☐ nicht möglich

g) Some children who simply live too far away from the nearest school miss ______________________ (have) fun with other children.

Infinitiv: ☐ möglich ☐ nicht möglich

Aufgabe 6: Vacation

***Gerund* oder Infinitiv? Setze die in Klammern angegebenen Verben in die richtige Form. Falls du beide Formen verwenden darfst, gib bitte auch beide Formen in der Lücke an.**

a) For many people vacation means ______________________________ ______________________________ (get away) from their usual surroundings.

b) Others prefer ______________________________ ______________________________ (continue) their usual routine.

c) Some tourists stop all their activities ______________________________ ______________________________ (stay) on a lonely island.

d) When they return home, they sometimes go on ______________________ ____________________ (live) a life that is completely different from before.

e) Some families love ______________________________ ______________________________ (spend) their vacation in clubs with an entertainment program.

f) Most people hate ______________________________ ________________ (think) about their problems while they are on vacation.

g) When they set off on their vacation, they meant ______________________ ______________________________ (enjoy) their time there, after all.

Aufgabe 7: An interview with a soccer star

Hier ist hier ein Interview mit Jacobs Lieblingsfußballer Kevin Kickwell. Setze die in Klammern angegebenen Verben im Infinitiv oder *gerund* in die Lücken ein.

a) Reporter: "Mr Kickwell, do you remember ______________________ (talk) to my colleague (*Kollegin*) six months ago?"

b) Kevin Kickwell: "Of course, I will never forget ______________________ (meet) that attractive young lady."

c) Reporter: "Well, at that time you meant ______________________ (switch) to a European club ..."

d) Kevin Kickwell: "Yes, I know. And then I went on ______________________ (play) for the USA."

e) Reporter: "So why did you try ______________________ (leave) the American league at all?"

f) Kevin Kickwell: "In a way, going to another country always means ______________________ (begin) a new life. This seemed like an interesting idea at the time."

g) Reporter: "Why did you stop ______________________ (think) about switching?"

h) Kevin Kickwell: "My old club tried ______________________ (offer) me more money to keep me. What more can I say?"

i) Reporter: "I see. So, thanks for your time, Mr Kickwell. Don't forget ______________________ (let) us know if you have any new plans."

j) Kevin Kickwell: "I'll call you then. And please remember ______________________ (say) hello to your nice colleague for me!"

Abschlusstest online 7

Super! Du hast das **Kapitel 7 – Das *gerund*** durchgearbeitet. Dabei hast du eine Verbform kennengelernt, die wie ein Nomen verwendet wird: das *gerund*. Außerdem hast du geübt, nach welchen Verben du das *gerund* benutzen musst und nach welchen den Infinitiv. Zum Glück gibt es auch welche, bei denen es egal ist, welche Form du wählst!

So funktioniert der Abschlusstest online:
Um deinen Lernerfolg zu überprüfen, kannst du nun die Abschlusstests machen. Gehe auf
https://www.klett-lerntraining.de/5N5D
und wähle das Kapitel und einen Test aus.

Welche Tests es gibt, siehst du unten in der Tabelle. Nach jedem Test bekommst du eine Auswertung.

Willst du immer im Blick haben, welche Themen du schon kannst oder was du besser wiederholen solltest? Dann schreibe deine Ergebnisse in die Tabelle.

Mein Ergebnis im Abschlusstest online – Kapitel 7

Thema	Mein Ergebnis
Das *gerund* als Subjekt oder Objekt	
Das *gerund* nach Präpositionen	
Der Gebrauch von Infinitiv und *gerund* nach bestimmten Verben	

8 Der Infinitiv

8.1 Der Infinitiv mit *to* nach Verb + Objekt

Um eine Bitte, einen Wunsch oder einen Befehl auszudrücken, kannst du im Englischen eine Konstruktion aus **Verb + Objekt + Infinitiv mit *to*** benutzen. Diese Konstruktion gebrauchst du auch für Aufforderungen in der indirekten Rede (siehe Kapitel 12.4, Seite 152).

Typische Einleitungsverben für diese Konstruktion sind z. B.:
to advise, to ask, to expect, to want, would like

Danach steht als Objekt die Person, die etwas tun soll.

	Verb	**Objekt**	**Infinitiv mit *to***	
My mother	**asks**	**me**	**to wash**	the dishes.
She	**expects**	**my brother**	**not to watch**	television.
She	**doesn't want**	**all of us**	**to sit there**	lazily.

Im Deutschen gibst du diese Konstruktion in der Regel mit einem dass-Satz oder dem Infinitiv wieder:
Meine Mutter bittet mich, **dass** ich das Geschirr abwasche.
Meine Mutter bittet mich, das Geschirr ab**zu**waschen.

Daher musst du unbedingt daran denken, dass im Englischen nach ***to want*** und ***would like*** nur der **Infinitiv** stehen darf: *that* darfst du nach diesen beiden Verben nicht verwenden!

Aufgabe 1: A midnight hike

Emmas Klasse unternimmt eine Nachtwanderung. Forme die Anweisungen des Lehrers in Infinitivkonstruktionen um.

a) You should take a flashlight (*Taschenlampe*) with you.

I want you to take a flashlight with you.

b) Listen to the noises of nocturnal animals (*Nachttiere*).

I expect you ______________________________

____

c) Don't laugh or scream loudly.

I don't want you ______________________________

____

d) Never leave the trail on your own.

I expect you ______________________________

____

e) Don't pick any wild flowers.

I don't want you ______________________________

____

f) All of you should wear warm jackets and sturdy (*feste*) boots.

I want all of you ______________________________

____

g) Don't use your cell phones (*Handys*) unless (*außer*) there is an emergency.

I don't want you ______________________________

____

Aufgabe 2: On a train

Emmas Klasse fährt Zug. Forme die Anweisungen des Schaffners (*train conductor*) in Infinitivkonstruktionen um.

a) All of you should behave well.

The conductor expects the students to behave well.

b) Don't lean out of the windows.

____

____

c) Don't leave any garbage (*Müll*) on the seats.

____

____

d) Don't get on other passengers' nerves.

____

____

e) Don't pull the emergency brake.

____

____

f) Don't eat burgers or ice-cream on the train.

____

____

g) Keep your voices down.

____

____

8.2 Der Infinitiv mit *to* nach Fragewörtern

Nebensätze mit den Modalverben *can*, *must* und *should* (oder einer ihrer Ersatzformen), die durch **Fragewörter** eingeleitet werden, kannst du verkürzen. Dazu verwendest du eine Konstruktion mit **Infinitiv + *to***. Das Modalverb kommt in der Infinitiv-Konstruktion nicht mehr vor.

	Fragewort	Nebensatz/ Infinitiv	
The student doesn't know	where	**he can find**	the cafeteria.
The student doesn't know	where	**to find**	the cafeteria.

Ausdrücke, nach denen du häufig einen solchen Infinitiv-Satz verwendest, sind z. B.:
to know, to wonder, to have no idea, to be sure

		Fragewort	Infinitiv mit *to*	
The student	wonders	**what**	**to tell**	his teacher.
He	didn't know	**when**	**to do**	his homework.

Im Deutschen musst du diese Konstruktion mit einem Modalverb wiedergeben, z. B.:
Der Schüler fragt sich, was er seinem Lehrer sagen **soll**.

Aufgabe 3: Lena in Los Angeles

Emmas und Jacobs deutsche Cousine Lena kennt sich in Los Angeles nicht aus. Schreibe ihre Fragen mithilfe der vorgegebenen Bausteine auf.

Lena She	wonders doesn't know has no idea isn't sure	how what where	a) to get to the beach. b) to do on a rainy day. c) to find the best burgers. d) to meet celebs (*Promis*). e) to buy cheap fashion. f) to expect from her vacation.

Aufgabe 4: At the airport

Wandle die unterstrichenen Satzteile in Infinitivkonstruktionen um. Schreibe die Sätze vollständig auf.

a) Many travelers don't know where they can park their cars.

Many travelers don't know where to park their cars.

b) They wonder which terminal they have to go to.

c) They aren't sure when they have to check in.

d) They have no idea what they can put into their hand luggage (*Handgepäck*).

e) They don't know what they shouldn't wear for the security check (*Sicherheitskontrolle*).

f) They aren't sure how long they have to wait for boarding.

Aufgabe 5: More questions about the airport

Wandle die Fragen der Reisenden in Sätze mit Infinitivkonstruktionen um. Beginne den Satz jeweils mit *The traveler*, *He* oder *She*. Wähle selbst ein einleitendes Verb und setze es ins *simple past*.

a) Where can I rent (*mieten*) a car?

She didn't know where to rent a car.

b) Who must I ask for information about the departure of my flight?

c) Where shall I report a theft (*Diebstahl*)?

d) How can I get to the viewing platform?

e) What must I do if I have missed my flight?

f) Where can I buy duty free (*zollfrei*) perfume?

g) What shall I do to get my lost luggage back?

h) Where must I go to find a doctor?

8.3 Der Infinitiv mit *to* nach *the first, the last, the only one* und Superlativen

Nach ***the first***, ***the last***, ***the only one*** und Superlativen (zweite Steigerungsform von Adjektiven, z. B. the fastest) kannst du den **Infinitiv mit *to*** verwenden:

		Infinitiv mit *to*	
Emma was Jacob was Emma wasn't Jacob wasn't	**the first** **the last** **the only girl** **the youngest boy**	**to arrive** **to come** **to eat** **to swim**	at school. into the classroom. two big burgers. a mile in the sea.

Beachte:
Nach *the only* musst du immer ein Nomen (z. B. the *only girl*) oder *one/ones* verwenden. *The first* und *the last* kannst du mit oder ohne Nomen gebrauchen. Andere Superlative verwendest du in der Regel mit Nomen.

Im Deutschen musst du diese Konstruktion mit einem Relativsatz wiedergeben, z. B.:
Emma war die Erste, <u>die in der Schule ankam</u>.

Aufgabe 6: A normal weekday morning

Schreibe mithilfe der vorgegebenen Bausteine Sätze mit Infinitiv auf.

Emma Jacob Mom Dad	was wasn't	the first the last the only one	a) to hear the alarm clock. b) to get dressed. c) to set the table for breakfast. d) to do a few sit-ups. e) to leave the house.

Aufgabe 7: Different qualities

Ergänze die Aussagen mit Infinitivkonstruktionen mithilfe der Angaben unten. Die Adjektive musst du noch in den Superlativ setzen.

first / cross the finish line (*Ziellinie*) – ~~good girl / give you advice~~ – realistic person / talk to – only student / work patiently on difficult problems aggressive boy / have an argument with – last / finish lunch open student / talk to – only student / tell really funny jokes young girl / graduate (*Abschluss machen*) from Jacob's school

a) Grace can understand other people's problems very well.

She is the best girl to give you advice.

b) Anthony runs very fast. He is always ______________________________

______________________________.

c) Ava is two years younger than her fellow classmates. She will be __________

______________________________.

d) Brittany doesn't like dreaming. She is ______________________________

______________________________.

e) Dave doesn't mind spending a lot of time on an exercise. He is __________

______________________________.

f) Andrew loves meeting new people. He is ______________________________

______________________________.

g) Katie eats very slowly. She is always ______________________________

______________________________.

h) Ryan can fight very hard for his rights. He is ______________________________

______________________________.

i) Carrie has a good sense of humor (*Humor*). She is ______________________________

______________________________.

Abschlusstest online 8

Glückwunsch! Du hast das **Kapitel 8 – Der Infinitiv** durchgearbeitet. Den Infinitiv kennst du ja schon lange als Grundform des Verbs. Hier ging es darum, wie du ihn einsetzen kannst, um bestimmte Dinge viel kürzer und geschickter auszudrücken.

So funktioniert der Abschlusstest online:
Um deinen Lernerfolg zu überprüfen, kannst du nun die Abschlusstests machen. Gehe auf
https://www.klett-lerntraining.de/5N5D
und wähle das Kapitel und einen Test aus.

Welche Tests es gibt, siehst du unten in der Tabelle. Nach jedem Test bekommst du eine Auswertung.

Willst du immer im Blick haben, welche Themen du schon kannst oder was du besser wiederholen solltest? Dann schreibe deine Ergebnisse in die Tabelle.

Mein Ergebnis im Abschlusstest online – Kapitel 8

Thema	Mein Ergebnis
Der Infinitiv mit *to* nach Verb + Objekt	
Der Infinitiv mit *to* nach Fragewörtern	
Der Infinitiv mit *to* nach *the first, the last, the only one* und Superlativen	

9 Das Passsiv

9.1 Die einfachen Passivformen

Der Gebrauch von Aktiv und Passiv

Wie im Deutschen unterscheidet man auch im Englischen zwischen Aktiv- und Passivformen. Der **Aktivsatz (*active voice*)** nennt den Handelnden. Er betont, wer etwas tut:
The boy **opens** the door.
→ Der Junge als Auslöser der Handlung steht im Mittelpunkt.

Beim **Passivsatz (*passive voice*)** wird die Handlung selbst betont. Es geht also darum, was mit einer Person oder Sache getan wird. Der Verursacher der Handlung ist unwichtig oder unbekannt (z. B. in Berichten oder Gebrauchsanweisungen).
The door **is opened**.
→ Die Tür, die geöffnet wird, steht im Mittelpunkt.

Vom Aktiv zum Passiv

Willst du einen Aktivsatz in einen Passivsatz umformen, musst du so vorgehen:

- Aus dem **Objekt** des Aktivsatzes machst du das **Subjekt** des Passivsatzes.
- Die aktive Verbform wandelst du in die **passive Verbform** um. Diese wird aus einer Form von ***to be*** und dem ***past participle*** gebildet (siehe dazu den Überblick auf der nächsten Seite).

- Willst du den Verursacher der Handlung nennen, hängst du diesen mit *by* an.
  Diesen Teil des Satzes nennt man *by-agent*.

	Subjekt	Prädikat	Objekt/by-agent
Aktiv	Tourists	take	many pictures.
Passiv	Many pictures	are taken	by tourists.

Die einfachen Passivformen im Überblick

Im Passiv setzt du das Verb *to be* in die entsprechende Zeitform, die du aus dem Aktiv kennst (siehe dazu Kapitel 1–5). Daran hängst du das *past participle* an.

simple present	*am/is/are + past participle*	it **is (not) made**
simple past	*was/were + past participle*	she **was (not) seen**
(*simple*) *present perfect*	*has been + past participle*	it **has (not) been written**
(*simple*) *past perfect*	*had been + past participle*	they **had (not) been used**
will-future	*will + be + past participle*	he **will (not) be heard**

Die Verneinung bildest du nach dem gleichen Muster wie bei den Aktivformen, indem du ***not*** an entsprechender Stelle einsetzt. Statt der angegebenen Langformen kannst du auch verneinte Kurzformen verwenden.

Aufgabe 1: How to make an American sandwich

Unterstreiche zunächst das Objekt in den Sätzen. Forme das Rezept anschließend in Passivsätze im *simple present* ohne *by-agent* um. Schreibe die Sätze auf.

a) First you need two slices (*Scheiben*) of white bread.

b) You put a little mayonnaise onto one slice of bread.

c) You lay some bacon on it.

d) You add some lettuce (*Salat*) and some tomato slices.

e) You top (*auf etwas legen; regelmäßiges Verb*) all that with the second slice of bread.

f) You cut the sandwich into four pieces.

g) You eat the sandwich with some potato chips.

Aufgabe 2: Somebody broke into school

Setze die in Klammern angegebenen Verben in die Passiv-Form des *simple past*.

a) The school ______________________________ (enter) through an open window in the gym.

b) The classroom doors ______________________________ (open) violently.

c) Some computer cables ______________________________ (hide) in a room in the basement (*Keller*).

d) Chairs and tables ______________________________ (put) in a huge pile (*Stapel*).

e) The classroom walls ______________________________ (cover) with colorful graffiti.

f) Hundreds of balloons (*Luftballons*) ______________________________ (leave) in the school building.

Aufgabe 3: Preparing for the movie award

Die Vorbereitungen für die Verleihung eines großen Filmpreises (*movie award*) sind im vollen Gange. Auf der Stichwortliste siehst du, was alles schon erledigt worden ist und was noch nicht. Bilde bejahte und verneinte Passivsätze im (*simple*) *present perfect*. Verwende *already* in den bejahten Sätzen und *not yet* in den verneinten Sätzen.

a) invite movie directors ✓

The movie directors have already been invited.

b) order food for buffet ✓

c) lay down the red carpet ✓

d) hold press conference ✗

e) buy 200 bottles of champagne ✓

f) write speeches about the winners of the awards ✗

Aufgabe 4: The Gold Rush

Setze die in Klammern stehenden Verben im *simple past* oder (*simple*) *past perfect* ins Passiv.

a) In the 19th century gold ______________________________

(discover) in California.

b) Because of that, the state ______________________________

(see) as a very attractive place by many poor people.

c) Rumors (*Gerüchte*) about gold ______________________________

(tell) for quite a while …

d) … until the first nugget (*Goldnugget*) ______________________________

(find) by a man called James Marshall.

e) Soon people from all over the world ______________________________

(bring) to California by the hope of finding gold, too.

Aufgabe 5: A green city of the future

In dieser Übung kannst du einen Blick in die Stadt der Zukunft werfen. Setze die in Klammern angegebenen Verben in das Passiv des *will-future*.

a) A lot of skyscrapers (*Hochhäuser*) ______________________________ (build).

b) Cars ______________________________ (not use) in the city center.

c) People on electric (*elektrisch*) bikes ______________________________ (see) everywhere.

d) Many trees ______________________________ (plant: *pflanzen, regelmäßiges Verb*) within the city.

e) The air ______________________________ (keep) very clean.

Aufgabe 6: The Walk of Fame

Forme die Sätze ins Passiv um und schreibe sie auf. Überlege jeweils, ob du den *by-agent* benötigst, damit der Satz im Passiv sinnvoll ist.

a) The Walk of Fame in Hollywood attracts (*anziehen, regelmäßiges Verb*) many visitors every year.

b) More than 2,000 stars on the sidewalk (*Gehsteig*) form that famous sight.

c) After some business people had discussed the idea for the Walk of Fame in the 1950s …

d) … money problems made the situation difficult for them.

e) The workers finished the first stars with artists' names in 1960.

f) Hollywood has added more than 2,000 stars since then.

g) Hollywood will honor (*ehren, regelmäßiges Verb*) many more artists with a star in the next century.

Aufgabe 7: The city of Los Angeles

Setze die Verben in Klammern im Passiv in die richtige Zeit: *simple present, simple past, (simple) present perfect, (simple) past perfect* oder *will-future*.

a) It ________________________ (often – say) that the area around Los Angeles is one of the most interesting metropolitan (*städtisch*) areas in the USA.

b) Los Angeles ________________________ (simply – call) LA by most people.

c) Did you know that LA ________________________ (make) a part of Mexico in the early 19th century?

d) This happened only a few years after the city ________________________ (found: *gründen, regelmäßiges Verb*).

e) In the middle of the 19th century, California ________________________ (buy) by the USA.

f) Since the 1920s Los Angeles ________________________ (know) for its very important entertainment industry.

g) In the late 20th century the city ________________________ (reported) to have a large crime problem (*Kriminalitätsproblem*).

h) Some people say that so far not enough ________________________ (do) to fight crime.

i) But it is certain that Los Angeles ________________________ (always – love) for its many museums and its important role in the media world.

9.2 Die Verlaufsformen im Passiv

Im Passiv gibt es neben den einfachen Formen auch zwei Verlaufsformen, das ***present progressive passive*** und das ***past progressive passive***.

Du setzt wieder das Verb *to be* in die entsprechende Zeit, und zwar nach den gleichen Regeln wie die entsprechenden Aktivformen (siehe dazu Kapitel 1.2, Seite 12, und 2.2, Seite 26). Dann hängst du das *past participle* an.

present progressive	*am/is/are + being + past participle*	it **is (not) being made**
past progressive	*was/were + being + past participle*	she **was (not) being seen**

Die Verneinung bildest du wie bei den Aktivformen, indem du ***not*** nach der jeweiligen Form von ***to be*** einsetzt. Statt der angegebenen Langformen kannst du (außer beim Infinitiv) auch verneinte Kurzformen verwenden.

Aufgabe 8: What is being done in Hollywood?

Bilde kurze Sätze mit der Verlaufsform des Passivs im *present tense* und schreibe sie auf:

a) actor - photograph

An actor is being photographed.

b) director - interview

c) articles- write

d) costumes - make

e) tickets - sell

f) movie - shoot

g) movie studio - open

h) ideas - discuss

Aufgabe 9: At the bowling center

Setze die in Klammern angegebenen Verben ins Passiv. Überlege dazu: Brauchst du das *simple present* oder das *present progressive*? Achte auch auf die richtige Stellung der vorgegebenen Adverbien!

a) This is how a game of bowling ______________________________ (usually – play):

b) Normally, a bowling alley (*Bahn*) ______________________________ (share) by several players.

c) First, the pins (*Kegel*) ______________________________ (set up) automatically.

d) Next, a bowling ball ______________________________ (choose) by the player.

e) Then the ball ______________________________ (roll: *rollen, regelmäßiges Verb*) down the bowling alley.

f) Let's see if everything ______________________________ (do) correctly at the bowling center in Los Angeles now.

g) How many points ______________________________ (score) on alley number 1 at this moment?

h) Don't worry, the points ______________________________ (always – count) by a computer program.

i) The points for alley number 1 ______________________________ (just – show) on a big screen (*Bildschirm*).

j) Look, the player ______________________________ (cheer on: *anfeuern, regelmäßiges Verb*) by his friends!

Aufgabe 10: Renovating (*renovieren*) the school

Als Emma gestern in die Schule kam, platzte sie mitten in Renovierungsarbeiten. Setze die in der Wörterschlange versteckten Verben der Reihe nach im *past progressive passive* in die Lücken ein.

paintwerchangebublayppIcleantztcarrybvbsetup

a) The walls ______________________________.

b) The curtains ______________________________.

c) A new carpet ______________________________.

d) Windows ______________________________.

e) New tables ______________________________ into the classrooms.

f) New computers ______________________________.

Aufgabe 11: On offer

Ordne die Buchstaben der Verben in Klammern und setze sie ins *present progressive passive* oder *past progressive passive*.

a) Fresh oranges ______________________________ (ffreo) at the market this season.

b) But the oranges that ______________________________ (slel) last year were much sweeter.

c) Last December many new products ______________________________ (retvadise).

d) This winter lots of electronics ______________________________ (owsh) in ads in magazines.

e) A pair of very stylish jeans ______________________________ (upt) into this shop window now.

f) They look better than the clothes which ______________________________ (retnsep) to customers last week.

Aufgabe 12: Stars on a lonely island

***Simple past passive* oder *past progressive passive*? Setze die in Klammern angegebenen Verben in die richtige Form.**

a) Last year a TV series about stars in the wilderness (*Wildnis*) ______________________________ (watch) by many people in the US.

b) A few actors and other famous people ______________________________ (fly) to a lonely island.

c) They ______________________________ (film) there 24 hours a day.

d) While the celebs (*Promis*) ______________________________ (watch) all the time,

e) they ______________________________ (place) into various (*verschiedene*) difficult situations.

f) First huts ______________________________ (build) out of wood without any tools (*Werkzeuge*).

g) Later dinner ______________________________ (prepare).

h) While fruit and berries (*Beeren*) ______________________________ (collected) by some, …

i) … insects (*Insekten*) ______________________________ (cook) by others.

j) Every day the stars ______________________________ (confront: *konfrontieren, regelmäßiges Verb*) with many more challenges.

k) Every week two celebs ______________________________ (choose) who had to fly back home.

l) In the end only one person ______________________________ (give) a prize for those hard weeks.

9.3 Der Infinitiv des Passivs mit und ohne *to*

Die Form des Infinitivs

Du kennst schon den **Infinitiv des Aktivs** mit und ohne ***to***:

(*to*) *make*, (*to*) *tell*, (*to*) *pay*

Die **Infinitivform** gibt es auch im **Passiv (*passive infinitive*)**, sie wird gebildet aus ***(to) be + past participle***:

(*to*) *be made*, (*to*) *be told*, (*to*) *be paid*

Gebrauch des Infinitivs Passiv mit *to*

Du verwendest den Infinitiv des Passivs mit *to* nach bestimmten Verben wie z. B.: *expect*, *hope*, *want*, *would like to*, *wish*, *seem*.

Subjekt	**Verb**	**Infinitiv Passiv mit *to***	
The tourists	**expect**	**to be shown**	all sights.
They	**would like**	**to be invited**	to a cup of tea.

Den englischen Infinitiv im Passiv musst du – je nach Satzzusammenhang – im Deutschen unterschiedlich wiedergeben:

- Die Touristen hoffen, **dass man** ihnen alle Sehenswürdigkeiten **zeigt**.
  → dass-Satz + man + Aktiv
- Sie würden gerne zu einer Tasse Tee **eingeladen werden**.
  → Infinitiv Passiv

Gebrauch des Infinitivs Passiv ohne *to*

Du verwendest den **Infinitiv Passiv ohne *to*** mit **modalen Hilfsverben** wie *can, could, may, might, must, should.*

Subjekt	**Modalverb**	**Infinitiv Passiv ohne *to***	
The pizza	**must**	**be eaten**	very hot.
The food	**can**	**be served**	in a few minutes.

Eine Ausnahme ist das Modalverb ***ought to***, das immer mit ***to*** konstruiert wird: The work **ought to be done** now.

Auch bei Konstruktionen mit Modalverb und Infinitiv Passiv hast du zwei Möglichkeiten für die Wiedergabe im Deutschen:

- Die Pizza muss **man** sehr heiß **essen**.
  → man + Aktiv
- Das Essen **kann** in ein paar Minuten **serviert werden**.
  → Infinitiv Passiv

Aufgabe 13: A good program

Was erwarten Fernsehzuschauer (*viewers*) von einem guten Fernsehprogramm? Bilde Sätze mit dem Infinitiv Passiv aus den Bausteinen. Die Vollverben musst du jeweils noch in die richtige Form setzen.

Beispiel: a) *People expect to be shown exciting action films.*

People Viewers They	expect hope want would like wish	to show to entertain (by) to inform about to tell about	a) exciting action films. b) important events. c) a romantic comedy. d) high-quality documentaries (*Dokumentarfilme*). e) politics. f) the economic situation. g) funny cartoons. h) thrillers.

Aufgabe 14: Hopes and dreams of future models

Was erhoffen sich die Teilnehmerinnen an einem Fernseh-Modelwettbewerb? Forme die mit *that* beginnenden Nebensätze in Konstruktionen mit dem Infinitiv Passiv um und schreibe sie auf.

a) The girls hope to be seen on TV by many people.

The girls hope that many people will see them on TV.

b) They hope that the judges (*Juroren*) will praise (*loben – regelmäßiges Verb*) them.

____

c) They expect that the hair stylists will give them a new look.

____

d) They hope that famous designers will dress them in expensive clothes.

____

e) They wish that the TV station will fly them to exotic (*exotisch*) places.

____

f) They expect that professionals (*Profis*) will photograph them.

____

g) They wish that the viewers will admire them.

____

h) They hope that a fashion magazine will choose them to be on the cover.

____

i) They hope that a good modeling agency will offer them a contract.

____

j) They expect that the judges will give them the first prize.

____

Aufgabe 15: Advice from the police

Oh Schreck! Bei den Sportslovers ist eingebrochen worden. Wie müssen sie sich nun verhalten? Formuliere die Verhaltensregeln der Polizei mithilfe der Modalverben unten und des Infinitivs Passiv um.

must – mustn't – ought to – ought not to – should – shouldn't

a) Call the police at once.

The police must be called at once.

b) Leave everything the way you found it.

c) Do not clean anything.

d) Do not enter a room if it is not necessary.

e) Write a list of the precious (*wertvoll*) things in your house.

Aufgabe 16: Jacob's housesitting job

Jacob hat einen kleinen Ferienjob übernommen: Er sieht im Haus einer befreundeten Familie nach dem Rechten. Schreibe Jacobs Aufgaben mithilfe von Modalverben und dem Infinitiv Passiv auf.

a) plants in the garden/give water

The plants in the garden must be given water.

b) grass/cut

____

c) cat/feed

____

d) windows/open and close again

____

e) mailbox/check

____

f) dog/walk

____

9.4 Das Passiv bei Verben mit zwei Objekten

Viele englische **Verben** kannnst du mit **zwei Objekten** verwenden, z. B.: *give, offer, promise, sell, send, show, teach, tell.*

In der Regel bezieht sich dann das eine Objekt auf eine Person, das andere auf eine Sache. Nennst du zuerst das Objekt, das sich auf die Sache bezieht, musst du das zweite Objekt mit ***to*** anschließen.

Subjekt	**Verb**	**1. Objekt**		**2. Objekt**
She	gave	him		a present.
She	gave	a present	to	him.

Zwei Möglichkeiten des Passivs

Bei Verben mit zwei Objekten hast du zwei Möglichkeiten, das Passiv zu bilden:

	Subjekt	**Verb**	**1. Objekt**	**2. Objekt**
Aktiv	He	told	**her**	**a story.**
1. Passivform: persönliches Passiv	**She**	was told	a story.	
2. Passivform	**A story**	was told	to her.	

- Beim **persönlichen Passiv** (*personal passive*) machst du das **Objekt**, das sich auf die **Person** bezieht, zum **Subjekt des Passivsatzes**. Diese Form kommt häufiger vor.
- Bei der anderen Möglichkeit machst du das **Objekt**, das sich auf die **Sache** bezieht, zum **Subjekt des Passivsatzes**. Die Person musst du dann mit ***to*** am Satzende anschließen.

Aufgabe 17: Friendly offers

Forme die Sätze ins Passiv um. Schreibe zu jedem Satz beide Möglichkeiten für das Passiv auf. Den *by-agent* brauchst du dabei nicht anzuhängen.

a) Jacob has offered Emma a special climbing tour.

Emma has been offered a special climbing tour.
A special climbing tour has been offered to Emma.

b) Jacob and Emma have promised Mom and Dad help at home and in the garden.

c) A shop has sent four vouchers (*Gutscheine*) for sportswear to the Sportslovers.

d) A neighbor has lent the family his camper van (*Wohnmobil*).

e) Jacob's friend has sold him an unused (*unbenutzt*) tent at a very good price.

f) Their uncle has shown Emma and Jacob a special place at the beach.

Aufgabe 18: Less friendly offers

Unterstreiche in den vorgegebenen Sätzen jeweils zuerst das Personenobjekt. Wandle die Sätze anschließend ins persönliche Passiv um. Den *by-agent* kannst du dabei weglassen.

a) A shop assistant sells a rain coat with a missing button (*Knopf*) to Jacob.

Jacob is sold a rain coat with a missing button.

b) Emma's friend sends her an e-mail with a computer virus.

c) Jacob's classmate tells Emma one of Jacob's secrets.

d) A travel company offers the Sportslovers a vacation at a hotel that doesn't exist.

e) A friend lends Emma a pair of broken ice skates.

f) A neighbor writes the Sportslovers letters of complaint (*Beschwerdebriefe*).

Aufgabe 19: An ad in a sports magazine

Setze zunächst aus den angegebenen Verben passende in die Lücken ein (du kannst sie auch mehrfach verwenden). Die Verben stehen bereits in der richtigen Zeitform. Wandle die Sätze anschließend ins persönliche Passiv um. Den *by-agent* benötigst du nicht in allen Sätzen.

will teach – ~~offer~~ – promise – will show – will tell – gives – offers – will send

a) We offer you the most exciting vacation (*Urlaub*) in your life.

You are offered the most exciting vacation in your life.

b) We ____________________ you weeks full of fun activities.

c) Our sports camp ____________________ you a chance to meet interesting people from all over the world.

d) Our hotel ____________________ all hobby surfers many great activities.

e) The world's best surfers ____________________ you useful tricks.

f) They ____________________ you about the secrets of surfing well during the daily lessons.

g) The experts on our hotline ____________________ you more about the whole travel package (*Reisepaket*).

h) They ____________________ you all about our prices and conditions (*Bedingungen*).

i) They ____________________ you our brochure with all the necessary information.

Abschlusstest online 9

Super! Du hast das **Kapitel 9 – Das Passiv** durchgearbeitet. Du hast gelernt, wie du Handlungen ausdrückst, deren Verursacher nicht wichtig oder sogar unbekannt ist. Das Passiv kannst du in fast allen Zeiten benutzen, die du auch schon im Aktiv kennst, und zwar mit *simple*- und *progressive*-Formen.

So funktioniert der Abschlusstest online:
Um deinen Lernerfolg zu überprüfen, kannst du nun die Abschlusstests machen. Gehe auf
https://www.klett-lerntraining.de/5N5D
und wähle das Kapitel und einen Test aus.

Welche Tests es gibt, siehst du unten in der Tabelle. Nach jedem Test bekommst du eine Auswertung.

Willst du immer im Blick haben, welche Themen du schon kannst oder was du besser wiederholen solltest? Dann schreibe deine Ergebnisse in die Tabelle.

Mein Ergebnis im Abschlusstest online – Kapitel 9

Thema	Mein Ergebnis
Die einfachen Passivformen	
Die Verlaufsformen im Passiv	
Der Infinitiv des Passivs mit und ohne *to*	
Das Passiv bei Verben mit zwei Objekten	

10 Relativsätze

10.1 Notwendige Relativsätze mit und ohne Relativpronomen

Relativsätze definieren das Wort, auf das sie sich beziehen, näher. Dass sie **notwendig** sind ***(defining relative clauses)***, erkennst du daran, dass du sie nicht einfach weglassen kannst, ohne den Sinn des Satzes zu verändern. Sie werden durch ein Relativpronomen eingeleitet, das **Objekt** oder **Subjekt** des Relativsatzes sein kann. Anders als im Deutschen steht vor notwendigen Relativsätzen im Englischen **kein Komma**.

Relativpronomen als Subjekt des Relativsatzes

Personen	**who/that**	Many people **who/that** live in New York use the subway every day.
Dinge	**which/that**	The boat **which/that** has the American flag on it is Mr Sportslover's boat.

Relativpronomen als Objekt des Relativsatzes

Personen	**whom/who/that**	The athlete **whom/who/that** you see in the picture is a famous runner.
Dinge	**which/that**	The skateboard **which/that** Jacob wants to buy is very expensive.

Whom wird in der förmlichen geschriebenen Sprache verwendet, ***who*** und ***that*** werden jedoch häufiger benutzt.

Die Relativpronomen können weggelassen werden, wenn sie Objekt des Relativsatzes sind (nur dann!). Diese Art der Relativsätze nennt man ***contact clauses***:

The athlete _ you can see in the picture is a famous runner.
The skateboard _ Jacob wants to buy is very expensive.

Das Relativpronomen *whose*

Das Relativpronomen ***whose*** steht immer vor einem Nomen. Es drückt aus, wem etwas gehört oder zu wem etwas gehört.

Personen	**whose**	The man **whose** sun-glasses broke is a well-known tennis player.
Dinge	**whose**	Running shoes **whose** material is special are often expensive.

Aufgabe 1: A quiz about the USA

Teste dein Wissen über die USA. In die erste Lücke musst du jeweils den gesuchten Namen (einer Stadt, eines Flusses, etc.) schreiben. In die zweite Lücke setzt du passende Relativpronomen ein. Gib immer alle Möglichkeiten für die Relativpronomen an!

a) _ _ _ _ _ _ _ _ _ _ is the part of Los Angeles ________________ is famous for its movie industry.

b) The _ _ _ _ _ _ _ _ _ _ _ _ is the river ________________ is longer than all the other American rivers.

c) The _ _ _ _ _ _ _ _ _ _ _ is the place ________________ is the home of the American President.

d) _ _ _ _ _ _ _ _ _ _ _ _ _ _ _ _ _ _ is the name of the man ________________ was the first American President.

e) _ _ _ _ _ _ _ _ is the woman ________________ sold more records and CDs than any other female (*weiblich*) singer.

Aufgabe 2: A quiz about sports

Gib in der ersten Lücke alle jeweils möglichen Relativpronomen an. Die gesuchte Bezeichnung für den Gegenstand oder die Person, um die es geht, gehört immer in die zweite Lücke. Kreuze außerdem für jeden Satz an, ob ein *contact clause* möglich ist.

a) The person ______________________ makes sure that a soccer game is fair is called a _ _ _ _ _ _ _ .

contact clause: ☐ möglich ☐ nicht möglich

b) The special glasses ______________________ you wear in the swimming pool are called _ _ _ _ _ _ _ .

contact clause: ☐ möglich ☐ nicht möglich

c) The thing ______________________ you hit the tennis ball with is called a _ _ _ _ _ _ .

contact clause: ☐ möglich ☐ nicht möglich

d) Someone ______________________ uses a board with four small wheels to do tricks in the air is called a _ _ _ _ _ _ .

contact clause: ☐ möglich ☐ nicht möglich

e) The prize ______________________ you can win at the Olympics is called a _ _ _ _ _ .

contact clause: ☐ möglich ☐ nicht möglich

Aufgabe 3: California and the Californians

Verbinde die Bausteine zu sinnvollen Sätzen. Schreibe sie auf und unterstreiche jeweils die Relativsätze.

a) California is a state b) A famous Californian c) Many scientists d) Many tourists	whose	1. career started in the 1970s is Arnold Schwarzenegger. 2. main interest is computers work in Silicon Valley. 3. hobby is surfing come to California. 4. climate (*Klima*) is very warm.

Aufgabe 4: Wanted!

Hier geht es um einen Bankraub. Verbinde die beiden Sätze jeweils mithilfe notwendiger Relativsätze. Bitte gib immer alle Möglichkeiten für die Relativpronomen an. Setze die Pronomen in Klammern, falls ein *contact clause* möglich ist.

a) The car was a big jeep. One of the gangsters was driving it.

The car (which/that) one of the gangsters was driving was a big jeep.

b) The man is very tall. His left eye is covered by a patch (*von einer Augenklappe verdeckt*).

____

____

c) The woman had a gun. She helped the man.

____

____

d) The passport is fake (*gefälscht*). The woman lost it in the bank.

____

____

e) The person wore a black mask. He was behind the wheel of the getaway car (*Fluchtauto*).

____

____

f) The sports bag was red and white. The robbers (*Räuber*) used it to carry the money out of the bank.

____

____

g) The robbery (*Raub*) happened in a bank. The clients are mostly rich.

____

____

10.2 Präpositionen im notwendigen Relativsatz

Manchmal steht im notwendigen Relativsatz eine Präposition. Du hast dann verschiedene Möglichkeiten für die Stellung der Präposition und die Verwendung des Relativpronomens.

Die **Präposition** steht im Relativsatz **hinter dem Verb**:

- Das Relativpronomen steht am Anfang des Relativsatzes:
  The boy **that/who** she is writing to lives in Germany.
- Du bildest einen *contact clause* und lässt das Relativpronomen weg:
  The boy she is writing to lives in Germany.

Die **Präposition** steht im Relativsatz **vor dem Relativpronomen**:
The boy **to whom** she is writing lives in Germany.
Diese Variante wird sehr selten verwendet. Es handelt sich dabei um förmlichen Sprachgebrauch, daher darfst du nur die beiden Relativpronomen *whom* oder *which* benutzen.

Aufgabe 5: Some facts about school

Ergänze jeweils die Relativpronomen (gib beide Möglichkeiten an) sowie eines der unten stehenden Verben mit Präposition.

write on – sit next to – keep in – talk to

a) A pencil case is a kind of small bag ______________________ you ______________________ your pens and pencils in.

b) A guidance teacher is a person ______________________ you can ______________________ in difficult situations.

c) A board is a large object ______________________ the teacher ______________________ during lessons.

d) The student ______________________ you ______________________ in the English lessons is your classmate.

Aufgabe 6: Special things on offer

Hier geht es um alltägliche Dinge, die an Wert gewinnen, weil berühmte Leute sie benutzt haben. Oft kannst du diese Dinge dann im Internet ersteigern. Bilde *contact clauses*. Beginne die Hauptsätze jeweils mit *You can find/buy* und schreibe sie auf.

a) a car – the winner of a model contest (*Wettbewerb*) drove around in it

   You can find a car the winner of a model contest drove around in.

b) a pair of soccer shoes – a world champion practiced in them

c) a house – a film star lived in it

d) a cup – a pop singer drank from it

e) a bag – the President's wife showed up (*erscheinen*) with it

f) a pen – a famous author wrote with it

g) a book – a princess drew a picture in it

Aufgabe 7: Formal English, please

Wandle die unterstrichenen Relativsätze in formelles Englisch um.

a) The manager of this shop is the only person I want to talk to.

   The manager of this shop is the only person to whom I want to talk.

b) The shop assistant I am angry with is not here today.

c) The product I want to complain (*sich beschweren*) about is your chocolate.

d) The shop assistant I bought it from had recommended the chocolate to me.

e) The problem I would like to talk about is that your chocolate is of very low quality.

10.3 Nicht-notwendige Relativsätze

Nicht-notwendige Relativsätze (*non-defining relative clauses*) liefern dir Zusatzinformationen zum Hauptsatz. Lässt man diese Art von Relativsätzen weg, ist der Hauptsatz immer noch verständlich.

American motels, which can be found across the whole country, attract many tourists.

Besonders häufig stehen solche Relativsätze nach Eigennamen:
Los Angeles, which is famous for its film industry, is a city in California.

Beim Gebrauch der nicht-notwendigen Relativsätze musst du einige wichtige Unterschiede zu den notwendigen Relativsätzen beachten:

	Notwendige Relativsätze	**Nicht-notwendige Relativsätze**
Kommasetzung	Keine Abtrennung durch Kommas vom Hauptsatz	Abtrennung durch Kommas vom Hauptsatz
Relativpronomen Personen	who(m)/that whose	who(m) whose
Relativpronomen Sachen	which/that whose	which whose
contact clause	möglich	nicht möglich

Achte bei Relativsätzen also besonders auf die **Kommasetzung**.
Denke außerdem immer daran, dass das Relativpronomen ***that*** bei den nicht-notwendigen Relativsätzen **nicht erlaubt** ist und dass du das Relativpronomen bei nicht-notwendigen Relativsätzen **nie weglassen** darfst!

Aufgabe 8: Las Vegas, city of entertainment

Notwendiger oder nicht-notwendiger Relativsatz? Setze alle nötigen Kommas und Relativpronomen ein. Falls du verschiedene Möglichkeiten für das Relativpronomen hast, genügt es, nur eine anzugeben.

a) Las Vegas ______________ is the biggest city in Nevada is well-known for its casinos.

b) It is a place ______________ millions of tourists visit every year.

c) The tourists often go to one of the many shows ______________ you can see there.

d) Elvis Presley ______________ performed in Las Vegas for several years is still alive there.

e) There are many actors and singers ______________ dress up as Elvis.

f) Maybe you have heard of the artists (*Künstler*) Siegfried and Roy ______________ both come from Germany.

g) They worked with white tigers ______________ are very beautiful but can also be very aggressive.

h) In a show a couple of years ago a tiger attacked Roy ______________ throat (*Hals*) was hurt very badly.

i) The wedding chapels (*Hochzeitskapellen*) of Las Vegas ______________ are a reason for many couples to come are famous all over the world.

j) Couples ______________ want to marry can do it very quickly there.

k) You can't imagine all the costumes and decorations (*Dekorationen*) ______________ they can choose from.

Aufgabe 9: Some facts about Washington, D.C.

Verbinde die beiden Sätze mithilfe von Relativsätzen und achte darauf, ob es sich um notwendige oder nicht-notwendige handelt. Falls du verschiedene Möglichkeiten für das Relativpronomen hast, genügt es, nur eine anzugeben.

a) Washington, D.C., isn't part of any state. It is the capital of the USA.

   Washington, D.C., which is the capital of the USA, isn't part of any state.

b) It is a fact that "D.C." is short for "District of Columbia." Many people don't know this fact.

c) About 600,000 people live in Washington. It is also the seat of the American government.

d) You may have seen a picture of the Capitol. It is a very famous building.

e) The city was named (*wurde benannt*) after the first President of the USA. He was called George Washington.

Aufgabe 10: More facts about Washington, D.C.

Ergänze eventuell fehlende Kommas in den Relativsätzen.
Kreuze alle Möglichkeiten an, die du für die einzelnen Lücken hast.

a) There is a lot of rain in Washington, a city ______ climate isn't very mild.

   ☐ who ☐ which ☐ that ☐ whose ☐ ohne Relativpronomen

b) The people ______ founded Washington settled close to the Potomac River.

   ☐ who ☐ which ☐ that ☐ whose ☐ ohne Relativpronomen

c) A building ______ many people want to see in Washington is the White House.

   ☐ who ☐ which ☐ that ☐ whose ☐ ohne Relativpronomen

Abschlusstest online 10

Klasse! Du hast das **Kapitel 10 – Relativsätze** durchgearbeitet. Dabei hast du dir noch einmal klargemacht, dass manche Relativsätze nicht weggelassen werden können, weil sonst der Rest des Satzes keinen Sinn mehr ergibt, andere aber nur zusätzliche Informationen liefern, die auch entfallen können. Im Englischen musst du dabei aufpassen, welche Relativpronomen du für welchen dieser Satztypen verwenden kannst.

So funktioniert der Abschlusstest online:
Um deinen Lernerfolg zu überprüfen, kannst du nun die Abschlusstests machen.
Gehe auf
https://www.klett-lerntraining.de/5N5D
und wähle das Kapitel und einen Test aus.

Welche Tests es gibt, siehst du unten in der Tabelle. Nach jedem Test bekommst du eine Auswertung.

Willst du immer im Blick haben, welche Themen du schon kannst oder was du besser wiederholen solltest? Dann schreibe deine Ergebnisse in die Tabelle.

Mein Ergebnis im Abschlusstest online – Kapitel 10

Thema	Mein Ergebnis
Notwendige Relativsätze mit und ohne Relativpronomen	
Präpositionen im notwendigen Relativsatz	
Nicht-notwendige Relativsätze	

11 Bedingungssätze

11.1 Typ 1: Erfüllbare Bedingungen

Gebrauch und Bildung von Bedingungssätzen (*if-clauses*)

Mit einem ***if*-Satz** im ***simple present*** drückst du eine **erfüllbare Bedingung** aus. Im dazugehörigen Hauptsatz steht, welche Folge sich für die Zukunft ergibt, falls diese Bedingung erfüllt wird.

Du kannst im **Hauptsatz** entweder ***will-future***, **Modalverben** oder den **Imperativ** (die Befehlsform) verwenden.

if*-Satz im *simple present	**Hauptsatz mit *will-future***
If Jacob **practices** very hard, **If** he **doesn't practice** very hard,	he **will become** a better climber. he **won't win** the competition.
if*-Satz im *simple present	**Hauptsatz mit Modalverben**
If you **go** to LA, **If** you **don't go** to LA,	you **can visit** a movie studio. you **can't take** pictures there.
if*-Satz im *simple present	**Hauptsatz mit Imperativ**
If you **have** your own computer, **If** you **don't have** your own computer,	**don't spend** too much time on the web. **use** one at school to do your research.

Der Hauptsatz kann auch vor dem *if*-Satz stehen. Dann entfällt das Komma.
She **will phone** me **if** there **are** any problems.

If und *when*

Das deutsche **wenn** wird im Englischen je nach Situation mit ***if*** (falls) oder ***when*** (zu dem Zeitpunkt, wenn) wiedergegeben. *If* und *when* stehen beide niemals mit dem *will-future* zusammen in einem Teilsatz!

If Emma watches the game, she will take pictures of the players.
→ Es ist möglich, aber nicht sicher, dass Emma das Spiel sieht.
When Emma watches the game, she will take pictures of the players.
→ Es ist sicher, dass Emma das Spiel sieht.

Aufgabe 1: Promises (Versprechen)

Manchmal wird in der Werbung ganz schön viel versprochen. Bilde mithilfe der Stichworte Bedingungssätze vom Typ 1.

a) drive this car/feel like a race driver

If you drive this car, you will feel like a race driver.

b) share these chocolate bars with your friends/have lots of fun

____

____

c) wear these jeans/look like a rock star

____

____

d) drink a cup of this tea/feel relaxed

____

____

e) use this shower gel/smell like a rose

____

____

f) have this drink/feel a lot more energetic (*voller Energie*)

____

____

Aufgabe 2: Ideas about the future

Bilde aus den vorgegebenen Bausteinen Bedingungssätze vom Typ 1. Setze die Verben bei Bedarf in die richtige Zeit. Im ersten Kasten findest du die Bedingung, im zweiten Kasten die Folge.

a) people only read e-books b) robots can answer all your questions c) computers can drive your car d) everybody pays for everything by credit card e) you can scan all the products at the supermarket yourself f) people write everything using computer keyboards	1. they can have long conversations with you 2. there aren't any more coins (*Münzen*) 3. they forget how to write by hand 4. nobody works at the check-out (*Kasse*) anymore 5. you can sleep behind the wheel 6. they don't need book shelves anymore

Aufgabe 3: Tips for all kinds of situations

Die folgenden Ratschläge erteilt die Kummerkastentante einer Zeitschrift. Bilde Bedingungssätze vom Typ 1 und verwende im Hauptsatz den Imperativ oder das Modalverb *should*.

a) feel lonely / join a sports club

If you feel lonely, join a sports club. / you should join a sports club.

b) dream of being famous / take part (*teilnehmen*) in a casting show

____

____

c) your best friend hurts you / tell him (her) how you feel

____

____

d) always get up too late / put a second alarm clock next to your bed

____

____

e) your room looks too boring / hang up some colorful posters

____

____

f) always fight with your family over which TV show to watch / let each family member pick one show a week

____

____

g) your teacher is always grumpy / ask him (her) about the reason

____

____

Aufgabe 4: What happens ...

If **oder** ***when*** **– was passt zu der im Bild dargestellten Situation?**

a) 

I will phone Cathy ______________ I get home.

b) 

______________ I finish this exercise, I will go for a run.

c) 

______________ Dad doesn't like this present, I will be very sad.

d) 

I won't take the bike ______________ it doesn't stop raining.

Aufgabe 5: A few days in the Rocky Mountains

Die Sportslovers wollen im nächsten Sommer zum Wandern in die Rocky Mountains fahren. Ergänze *if* oder *when* und setze die in Klammern angegebenen Verben in die richtige Zeit.

a) ______________ the Sportslovers ____________________________ (arrive) in the Rocky Mountains, they ___________________ (try) to get a place at their favorite campground (*Campingplatz*) close to the lake.

b) ________ it ____________________________ (be) full, the family ____________________________ (go) to a campground next to the river.

c) ______________ the Sportslovers ____________________________ (go) hiking in the Rocky Mountains next summer, they ____________________________ (watch out) for animals.

d) They ____________________________ (can take) some nice pictures of elk (*Wapiti-Hirsche*) ______________ they ____________________________ (be) lucky.

e) ______________ they ____________________________ (see) a bear, they ____________________________ (stand) still.

f) ______________ the bear ____________________________ (take) away their food, they ____________________________ (not try) to get it back.

g) ______________ the Sportslovers ____________________________ (pack) their bags for the Rocky Mountains, they ____________________________ (must remember) to take enough drinking water with them.

h) It ____________________________ (can be) difficult to find fresh water ______________ you ____________________________ (walk) through the Rocky Mountains.

i) ______________ the Sportslovers ____________________________ (enjoy) their trip to the Rocky Mountains, they ____________________________ (return) soon.

11.2 Typ 2: Theoretisch erfüllbare Bedingungen

Mit einem ***if*-Satz** im ***simple past*** drückst du eine **Bedingung** aus, die nur **theoretisch erfüllt** werden kann. Das *simple past* bezieht sich hier nicht auf die Vergangenheit, sondern drückt aus, dass etwas sehr unwahrscheinlich ist:

If I **got** more pocket-money, I would buy new running shoes.
→ Eine Taschengelderhöhung ist zwar möglich, aber sehr unwahrscheinlich.

Im dazugehörigen **Hauptsatz** steht, welche **Folge** sich ergäbe, falls die Bedingung einträte. Du gebrauchst im **Hauptsatz *would + Infinitiv***. Diese Form nennt man auch ***conditional I***.
Außerdem kannst du auch ***could + Infinitiv*** oder ***might + Infinitiv*** im Hauptsatz verwenden.

if*-Satz im *simple past	**Hauptsatz**	
If I **had** an umbrella, **If** the sea **wasn't** so cold,	I **wouldn't get** wet. I **would go** swimming.	*would* + Infinitiv
If I **had** his mail address, **If** he **had** my phone number,	I **could write** to him. he **might call** me.	*could/might* + Infinitiv

Sowohl im *if*-Satz als auch im Hauptsatz können bejahte und verneinte Formen stehen. Der Hauptsatz kann auch hier vor dem *if*-Satz stehen:
My friends **would laugh** so hard **if** they **saw** me now.

Beachte:
Im *if*-Satz kann die Form *were* auch für die 1. und 3. Person Singular benutzt werden:
if I **was**/if I **were** (*wenn ich wäre*)
if he/she/it **was**/if he/she/it **were** (*wenn er/sie/es wäre*)

Aufgabe 6: If I was …

Bilde aus den vorgegebenen Bausteinen Bedingungssätze vom Typ 2. Beginne jeweils mit *If I was*. Verwende im Hauptsatz *would* oder *could*.

Beispiel: a) *If I was a millionaire, I would/could live in a big mansion with a pool.*

a) ~~a millionaire (*Millionär*)~~ b) a pilot c) a cowboy/cowgirl d) a scientist e) a teacher f) a manager	see the whole world ~~live in a big mansion (*Villa*) with a pool~~ invent (*erfinden*) a robot that does my homework never shout at my students work in an office in a skyscraper (*Wolkenkratzer*) spend the whole day on horseback (*auf dem Pferd*)

Aufgabe 7: The Sportslovers' dreams

Bilde Bedingungssätze vom Typ 2. Setze die in Klammern vorgegebenen Verben in die richtige Form.

a) If Emma ______________________ (have) a dog,
she ______________________ (walk) it every day.

b) Jacob ______________________ (be) in a band
if he ______________________ (can play) the guitar.

c) Mom ______________________ (learn) Spanish
if she ______________________ (not work) so much.

d) If Dad ______________________ (own) a faster boat,
he ______________________ (sail) across the Atlantic.

Aufgabe 8: What would you do?

Du hast je zwei Möglichkeiten, wie du dich in einer bestimmten Situation entscheiden würdest. Bilde Bedingungssätze vom Typ 2, die deine Meinung wiedergeben und schreibe sie auf.

a) You get too much change at the supermarket checkout counter. Do you keep it or give it back?

If I got too much change at the supermarket checkout counter, I wouldn't keep it. I would give it back.

b) Your parents read the text messages on your mobile phone. Do you accept (*akzeptieren*) it or do you start an argument with them?

c) Your classmates say bad things about your best friend. Do you tell your friend or do you keep the whole thing to yourself?

d) Your teacher treats (*behandeln*) your classmate unfairly (*ungerecht*). Do you speak up (*sich einsetzen*) for him/her or do you keep quiet?

e) You are late for school simply because you were walking too slowly. Do you tell the teacher the truth or do you tell him/her a lie?

f) Your parents are away over the week-end. Do you study for your English test or do you have a party?

g) You get a text message from a secret admirer (*Verehrer*). Do you want to find out who he/she is, or do you forget about it?

h) Your neighbor at school is very good at English. Do you copy from him/her while taking a test or do you write down your own ideas?

Aufgabe 9: Everyday situations

Kreuze jeweils den Satz an, der zu der dargestellten Situation passt. Überlege dazu: Ist die Bedingung erfüllbar und wahrscheinlich, oder ist es eher unwahrscheinlich, dass sie eintritt?

☐ If it isn't seven o'clock, Emma won't get up. She will stay in bed.

☐ If it wasn't seven o'clock, Emma wouldn't get up. She would stay in bed.

☐ If the cake is good, Jacob will eat another piece.

☐ If the cake was good, Jacob would eat another piece.

☐ If Jacob isn't such a good runner, he will not win the race.

☐ If Jacob wasn't such a good runner, he wouldn't win the race.

☐ If Emma doesn't catch the bus, she will wait for the next one.

☐ If Emma didn't catch the bus, she would wait for the next one.

☐ If Emma is at the beach, she will go for a swim.

☐ If Emma was at the beach, she would go for a swim.

11.3 Typ 3: Unerfüllbare Bedingungen

Mit einem ***if*-Satz** im ***past perfect*** drückst du eine **Bedingung** aus, die in der Vergangenheit liegt und deshalb nicht mehr erfüllt werden kann. Es geht also um eine Situation, die du nachträglich nicht mehr ändern oder beeinflussen kannst.

If he **hadn't been** ill, he wouldn't have missed so much at school.
→ Wäre er nicht krank gewesen, hätte er in der Schule nicht so viel verpasst. Daran lässt sich aber nichts mehr ändern.

Im dazugehörigen **Hauptsatz** steht, welche **Folge** sich ergeben hätte, falls die Bedingung eingetreten wäre. Du gebrauchst im **Hauptsatz *would* + *have* + *past participle***. Diese Form nennt man auch conditional II. Außerdem kannst du auch ***could* + *have* + *past participle*** im Hauptsatz verwenden.

if*-Satz im *simple past	**Hauptsatz mit** ***would* + *have* + *past participle***
If she **had left** the party later, **If** he **hadn't done** his homework,	she **wouldn't have caught** the last bus. he **would have been** in trouble.
if*-Satz im *simple past	**Hauptsatz mit** ***could* + *have* + *past participle***
If she **hadn't lost** my number, **If** he **had tried** to phone me last week,	she **could have called** me. he **couldn't have reached** me.

Sowohl im *if*-Satz als auch im Hauptsatz können bejahte und verneinte Formen stehen.

Achtung:
Die Kurzform ***'d*** kann sowohl für ***had*** als auch für ***would*** stehen. Du entgehst hier aber leicht der Verwechslungsgefahr, wenn du beachtest, dass ***would* nicht** im ***if*-Satz** stehen darf!

Aufgabe 10: A Californian surfer's accident

Bilde Bedingungssätze vom Typ 3. Setze dazu die in Klammern angegebenen Verben in die richtige Form.

a) If John Supersurf ______________________ (listen) to his friends, he ______________________ (stay) at home on that stormy day.

b) If he ______________________ (not try) to surf, he ______________________ (not have) that terrible accident.

c) John ______________________ (not fall) off his surfboard if he ______________________ (not be) so tired.

d) If there ______________________ (not be) such high waves, John ______________________ (not hit) his head on the board.

e) If he ______________________ (not lose) any blood, the shark ______________________ (not smell) it.

f) If the shark ______________________ (not find) John, it ______________________ (not attack) him.

g) If John's friends ______________________ (not worry) about him, they ______________________ (not call) the coast guard (*Küstenwache*).

h) John ______________________ (not survive) if the coast guard ______________________ (not save) him.

i) If a journalist ______________________ (not hear) about that story, she ______________________ (not write) an article about it.

Aufgabe 11: Will, would or would have?

Bilde Bedingungssätze mithilfe der Angaben zu den einzelnen Bildern und schreibe sie auf. Entscheide je nach Situation, ob du Sätze vom Typ 1, 2 oder 3 bilden musst. Der erste Teil der Angabe bezieht sich jeweils auf die Bedingung, der zweite auf die Folge.

Beispiel: a) *If there was snow, Jacob could throw a snowball at his sister.*

Jacob: there be snow / can throw a snowball at his sister

Emma: go slower / not fall down in the street

Mr Sportslover: get as many mails as yesterday / take him the whole afternoon to read them

Mrs Sportslover: get home in time/ watch her favorite soap on TV

Emma: Jacob not be her brother/not lend him her new jacket

Jacob: prepare better for the test/have a better grade

Abschlusstest online 11

Na, alles durchgearbeitet? In **Kapitel 11 – Bedingungssätze** hast du dir Gedanken gemacht über die Fragen: „Was ist eigentlich, wenn …?", „Was wäre, wenn …?" und „Was wäre gewesen, wenn …?". Und bestimmt hast du dir gemerkt, dass *will* und *would* niemals, niemals, niemals im *if*-Satz stehen!

So funktioniert der Abschlusstest online:
Um deinen Lernerfolg zu überprüfen, kannst du nun die Abschlusstests machen. Gehe auf
https://www.klett-lerntraining.de/5N5D
und wähle das Kapitel und einen Test aus.

Welche Tests es gibt, siehst du unten in der Tabelle. Nach jedem Test bekommst du eine Auswertung.

Willst du immer im Blick haben, welche Themen du schon kannst oder was du besser wiederholen solltest? Dann schreibe deine Ergebnisse in die Tabelle.

Mein Ergebnis im Abschlusstest online – Kapitel 11

Thema	Mein Ergebnis
Typ 1: Erfüllbare Bedingungen	
Typ 2: Theoretisch erfüllbare Bedingungen	
Typ 3: Unerfüllbare Bedingungen	

12 Die indirekte Rede

12.1 Indirekte Aussagesätze

Direkte und indirekte Rede

Die indirekte Rede (*reported speech; indirect speech*) gebrauchst du, genau wie im Deutschen, wenn du wiedergeben willst, was jemand gesagt hat.

Direkte Rede	She says: "I like this movie very much."
Indirekte Rede	She said (that) she liked that movie very much.

Meistens leitest du die indirekte Rede mit **Verben des Sagens und Denkens** ein, wie z. B.:
say, tell somebody, explain, mention, think, hope, promise

Die indirekte Rede wird dann mit einem Satz mit *that* angeschlossen (Du darfst das *that* aber auch weglassen.). Beachte, dass zwischen Einleitungssatz und indirekter Rede, anders als im Deutschen, kein Komma steht!

Häufig musst du in der indirekten Rede die Personalpronomen anpassen. Im oberen Beispiel wird z. B. *I* zu *she*.

Einleitendes Verb im *present tense*

Steht das einleitende Verb im *present tense*, dann behältst du die Zeitformen der direkten Rede in der indirekten Rede bei.

Direkte Rede	He says: "The weather **is** fine."
Indirekte Rede	He **says** the weather **is** fine.

Einleitendes Verb im *past tense*

Steht das einleitende Verb der indirekten Rede im *past tense*, dann musst du die Zeitformen der direkten Rede in der indirekten Rede verändern. Man spricht hier von einer Verschiebung der Zeiten (*tense shift*).

Direkte Rede	She says: "I **play** tennis every week."
Indirekte Rede	She **said** she **played** tennis every week.

Der indirekt wiedergegebene Satz wird also in die Vergangenheit „verschoben": *simple present* wird zu *simple past*.

Die Verschiebung der Zeiten folgt sowohl für die einfachen Formen (*simple forms*) wie auch für die Verlaufsformen (*progressive forms*) den gleichen Regeln:

Direkte Rede		**Indirekte Rede**
simple present	→	simple past
present progressive	→	past progressive
simple past	→	past perfect
past progressive	→	past perfect progressive
present perfect	→	past perfect
present perfect progressive	→	past perfect progressive
past perfect	→	past perfect **(bleibt!)**
past perfect progressive	→	past perfect progressive **(bleibt!)**
will	→	would
can	→	could

Bei der Umformung von direkter Rede in die indirekte Rede können folgende Formen nicht verändert werden:
- *past perfect*
- *past perfect progressive*
- *could*, *would* und *should*

Aufgabe 1: An exchange student in Jacob's class

In Jacobs Klasse sind heute deutsche Austauschschüler zu Gast. Einer von ihnen, Benjamin, stellt sich vor. Gib seine Aussagen in indirekter Rede wieder. Suche dir jeweils ein einleitendes Verb aus und setze es ins *simple present*.

say – explain –mention – add – tell the students – say – hope

a) "I am fourteen years old."

Benjamin says (that) he is fourteen years old.

b) "I come from a small town near Frankfurt."

c) "I have been learning English for four years."

d) "Before I came here on the exchange …

e) … I had never been to the USA."

f) "I have already learned a lot about California."

g) "I really love the American way of life."

h) "I will come back to LA one day."

Aufgabe 2: Talking about Benjamin again

Verwende noch einmal die Angaben aus Aufgabe 1. Setze das einleitende Verb dieses Mal ins *simple past* und schreibe die Sätze auf.

Beispiel: a) *Benjamin said (that) he was fourteen years old.*

Aufgabe 3: An accident in Emma's class

Schreibe Emmas Bericht in indirekter Rede auf. Setze die einleitenden Verben, die in Klammern angegeben sind, ins *simple past*.

a) (say): "Matt had his basketball with him in the classroom."

Emma said (that) Matt had had his basketball with him in the classroom.

b) (add): "He wanted to play with Luke between classes."

c) (explain): "Matt threw the ball at Luke."

d) (say): "He accidentally (*versehentlich*) hit the lamp."

e) (add): "Luckily nobody was hurt."

Aufgabe 4: Discussing tattoos

Jacob möchte gerne ein kleines Tattoo, seine Mutter ist jedoch absolut dagegen. Gib die Argumente der beiden in indirekter Rede wieder. Das einleitende Verb setzt du jeweils ins *simple past*.

a) Jacob: "I want to get a small tattoo on my back."

b) Mom: "You are much too young to get a tattoo."

c) Jacob: "People who are much younger have already gotten tattoos."

d) Mom: "I don't care what other people do."

e) Jacob: "There are simply no good reasons for your decision."

f) Mom: "Tattoos are bad for your health."

g) Jacob: "The tattoo studio uses only safe tattoo inks (*Farben*)."

h) Mom: "If the studio isn't clean, you will still (*dennoch*) risk infections."

i) Jacob: "You can come with me to the studio and see if it is clean."

j) Mom: "It will be difficult to get a job if you have a tattoo."

k) Jacob: "Nobody will see my tattoo if it is on my back."

l) Mom: "Maybe you won't like the tattoo anymore when you're older."

m) Jacob: "If this is the case, I can get rid of my tattoo."

n) Mom: "I've had enough. I will never allow you to get a tattoo."

12.2 Zeitangaben in der indirekten Rede

Beibehaltung der Zeitangabe

Häufig kommen in der direkten Rede Zeitangaben vor, die sich auf einen bestimmten Tag beziehen, wie *yesterday*, *today* oder *tomorrow*. Berichtest du noch am selben Tag in indirekter Rede darüber, so ändert sich die Zeitangabe nicht.

Emma erzählt z. B. Jacob in der Schule:
"I will write a math test **tomorrow**."
Jacob berichtet seinen Eltern noch am gleichen Tag:
"Emma told me she would write a math test **tomorrow**."

Auch Zeitangaben, die sich auf einen bestimmten Monat oder ein bestimmtes Jahr beziehen, behältst du bei, wenn der betreffende Monat oder das Jahr noch nicht vorbei sind.

Veränderung der Zeitangabe

Meist ist der Zeitpunkt, auf den sich Zeitangaben in der indirekten Rede beziehen, jedoch schon vorüber, wenn darüber berichtet wird.

Erzählt Jacob seinen Eltern z. B. erst einige Tage später von Emmas Klassenarbeit, würde er das so ausdrücken:
"(A few days ago) Emma told me she would write a math test **that day**."

Die Zeitangaben der direkten Rede werden so verändert:

Direkte Rede		**Indirekte Rede**
(a month) ago	→	(a month) before/earlier
last (year)	→	(a year) before
yesterday	→	the day before
today	→	that day
tonight	→	that evening
tomorrow	→	the next/following day
next year	→	the following year

Weitere Veränderungen in der indirekten Rede

Je nach Satzzusammenhang können weitere Veränderungen in der indirekten Rede nötig sein. Die häufigsten sind:

Direkte Rede		Indirekte Rede
this	→	that
here	→	there

Aufgabe 5: Talking about Benjamin's time in LA

Benjamin, einer der deutschen Austauschschüler in Jacobs Klasse, hat einen Cousin in Amerika. Er telefoniert mit ihm und erzählt ihm von dem Austausch. Schreibe auf, was der Cousin am gleichen Abend seinen Eltern berichtet.

a) "We have already done so much since last week."

Benjamin said (that) they had already done so much since last week.

b) "Yesterday we went to Venice Beach."

c) "This place is simply fantastic."

d) "Today we could choose between different activitities at school."

e) "So I went to American football training this afternoon."

f) "Jacob, a boy from school, has invited me to a barbecue party tonight."

g) "I am going to stay with Jacob's family until tomorrow."

h) "Tomorrow I am going to take a diving (*Tauchen*) lesson."

i) "I am also looking forward to going to the school dance next week-end."

Aufgabe 6: Passing on (weitergeben) information

Verwende noch einmal die Angaben aus Aufgabe 5. Schreibe auf, was der Cousin eine Woche später seiner Schwester über den Anruf erzählt.

Beispiel: a) *Benjamin said (that) they had already done so much since the week before.*

12.3 Indirekte Fragen

Die Regeln für die Verwendung der Zeiten in der indirekten Rede kennst du bereits von den Aussagesätzen (siehe Kapitel 12.1). Diese Regeln gelten auch für **Fragen in der indirekten Rede** (*indirect questions*). Typische Einleitungsverben für indirekte Fragen sind *to ask* und *to want to know*.

Entscheidungsfragen in der indirekten Rede

Entscheidungsfragen (Fragen ohne Fragewort) werden in der indirekten Rede durch ***if*** oder ***whether*** eingeleitet:

Direkte Rede	Indirekte Rede
Emma: "**Do** you **play** tennis, Lisa?"	Emma asked Lisa **if** she **played** tennis.
Emma: "**Did** you **watch** the tennis match on TV yesterday?"	She wanted to know **if** Lisa **had watched** the tennis match on TV the day before.

Die Satzstellung in der indirekten Frage ist genau wie die **Satzstellung im Aussagesatz**. Auch verwendest du in der indirekten Frage die Verbformen wie im Aussagesatz, d.h. du benutzt bei bejahten Verbformen keine Umschreibung mit *do/did*.

Ergänzungsfragen in der indirekten Rede

Formst du **Ergänzungsfragen** (Fragen mit Fragewort) in die indirekte Rede um, behältst du das **Fragewort** auch in der indirekten Frage bei. Auch hier entsprechen **Satzstellung** und Verbform dem **Aussagesatz**:

Direkte Rede	Indirekte Rede
Lisa: "**Where do** you **go** swimming, Emma?"	Lisa asked Emma **where** she **went** swimming.
Lisa: "**When did** you **win** your last swimming competition?"	She wanted to know **when** Emma **had won** her last swimming competition.

Aufgabe 7: Questions to Benjamin

Die Klasse von Jacob hat viele Fragen an den deutschen Austauschschüler Benjamin. Gib sie in indirekter Rede wieder.

a) "Do you like our school?"

The students asked *if/whether Benjamin liked their school.*

b) "Do you have a girlfriend?"

They wanted to know ______________________________

____

c) "Have you ever had a date (*Verabredung*) with an American girl?"

The boys and girls asked ______________________________

____

d) "Are there any differences between Germans and Americans?"

Jacob's classmates wanted to find out ______________________________

____

e) "Have you ever been to a school dance?"

They asked ______________________________

____

f) "Have you seen a lot of California yet?"

One of their questions was ______________________________

____

g) "Do you know any Americans in Europe?"

The students were interested in finding out ______________________________

____

Aufgabe 8: More questions for Benjamin

Direkt nachdem Benjamin in den USA angekommen ist, hat auch sein amerikanischer Cousin einige Fragen an ihn. Schreibe diese in indirekter Rede auf. Das einleitende Verb setzt du dazu immer ins *simple past*.

a) "Did you have any problems during the flight?"

Benjamin's cousin asked if/whether he had had any problems during the flight.

b) "Did you sleep during the flight?"

c) "Did you get a seat next to your friend on the plane?"

d) "Was the food on board the plane all right?"

e) "Did the stewardess speak German?"

f) "Did your host family meet you at the airport in LA?"

g) "Do you feel comfortable (*wohl*) with your host family?"

h) "Are you sharing a room with your host brother?"

Aufgabe 9: Questions not to ask

Hier findest du einige Fragen, die du bei einer Verabredung besser nicht stellen solltest. Setze sie in die indirekte Rede. Beginne deine Sätze jeweils mit *Never ask* ... Denke daran, dass du in diesem Fall die Zeit nicht verschiebst.

a) "Why are you wearing such an awful T-shirt?"

Never ask why your date (Datingpartner) is wearing such an awful T-shirt.

b) "Where did you get your terrible haircut?"

c) "Why can't you tell me anything more interesting?"

d) "When can I go home?"

e) "Why did you choose such a boring movie?"

f) "When will you stop getting on my nerves?"

g) "What can I do to finish this date as quickly as possible?"

h) "Why didn't I say no when you asked me out?"

Aufgabe 10: Benjamin's date

Benjamin stellt bei seiner Verabredung mit Nicky, einem Mädchen aus Jacobs Klasse, die richtigen Fragen. Gib diese in indirekter Rede wieder. Setze das einleitende Verb ins *simple past*.

a) "What would you like to drink?"

Benjamin asked Nicky what she would like to drink.

b) "Where did you buy this fantastic dress?"

c) "What do you want to know about me?"

d) "What do you usually do on week-ends?"

e) "How did you learn to speak German so well?"

f) "Who do you hang out with at school?"

g) "What kind of movies do you like?"

h) "When will I see you again?"

Aufgabe 11: Questions after a traffic accident

Hier geht es um typische Fragen eines Polizisten direkt nach einem Verkehrsunfall. Diesmal musst du die indirekte Rede in direkte Rede „zurückübersetzen". Kreuze die Version an, die dem indirekten Satz am besten entspricht.

a) He wanted to know who had been driving the car at the time of the accident.

☐ "Who was driving the car at the time of the accident?"

☐ "Who has been driving the car at the time of the accident?"

b) He asked if anybody had been injured (*verletzt*).

☐ "Is anybody injured?"

☐ "Has anybody been injured?"

c) He tried to find out why the man hadn't stopped at the traffic light (*Ampel*).

☐ "Why didn't you stop at the traffic light?"

☐ "Why did you stop at the traffic light?"

12.4 Indirekte Aufforderungssätze

Befehle, Bitten und Aufforderungen kannst du ebenfalls in der indirekten Rede wiedergeben (*indirect commands*). Dazu verwendest du eine **Infinitivkonstruktion mit *to*** (siehe auch Kapitel 8.1). Diese besteht aus **Verb + Objekt + Infinitiv mit *to***. Die verneinte Form des Infinitivs lautet ***not to***:

	Verb	**Objekt**	**Infinitiv mit *to***	
The teacher	asked	the students	**to be**	quiet.
He	advised	them	**not to**	run around.

Als Objekt steht immer die Person, an die sich die Aufforderung richtet.

Indirekte Aufforderungssätze werden häufig durch Verben wie *tell*, *ask*, *warn*, *advise* und *remind* eingeleitet.

Direkte Rede	**Indirekte Rede**
Teacher: "Put your exercise books back into your bags, please."	The teacher **told** the students **to put** their exercise books back into their bags.
Teacher: "Don't talk to your neighbor during the test."	He **warned** them **not to talk** to their neighbors during the test.

Auch bei indirekten Aufforderungssätzen musst du darauf achten, dass du Personalpronomen und Zeitangaben häufig an den veränderten Standpunkt anpassen musst:

Direkte Rede	**Indirekte Rede**
Teacher: "Don't forget to prepare for **your** test **tomorrow**."	The teacher reminded the students not to forget to prepare for **their** test **the following day**.

Aufgabe 12: How to behave at school

Jacobs Lehrerin besteht darauf, dass bestimmte Regeln in ihrem Unterricht eingehalten werden. Forme diese Regeln in indirekte Aufforderungssätze um, indem du die Sätze ergänzt.

a) "Show respect (*Respekt*) to your fellow classmates."

The teacher asked the students …

b) "Don't distract each other."

She advised them …

c) "Don't talk if it's not your turn."

She told them …

d) "Never laugh about a wrong answer."

She reminded them …

e) "Don't tell me lies about your missing homework."

She warned them …

f) "Don't hit each other."

She told them …

g) "Keep the classroom clean and tidy."

She asked them …

h) "Don't make fun of your fellow classmates."

She advised them …

i) "Come to the lessons on time."

She reminded them …

j) "Turn off your cell phones (*Handys*) during lessons."

She warned them …

k) "Don't wear caps (*Kappen*) or hats in the classroom."

She asked them …

Aufgabe 13: A school exchange with Germany

Bald fährt eine Gruppe von Schülern an Emmas und Jacobs Schule zu einem Austausch nach Deutschland. Der Lehrer Mr Niceguy erteilt noch einmal einige Anweisungen. Forme diese in indirekte Aufforderungssätze um, das einleitende Verb setzt du bitte immer ins *simple past*.

a) "Let me know about any problems."

Mr Niceguy advised the students to let him know about any problems.

b) "Remember that many things are different in Germany."

____

c) "Always be polite to your host families."

____

d) "Don't behave selfishly."

____

e) "Don't break your host parents' rules."

____

f) "Take warm clothes with you."

____

g) "Take part in (*teilnehmen an*) your host families' activities."

____

h) "Bring your host families some small presents."

____

i) "Try to speak some simple German sentences."

____

j) "Don't forget your dictionaries."

____

Abschlusstest online 12

Geschafft! Du hast das **Kapitel 12 – Die indirekte Rede** durchgearbeitet. Jetzt weißt du, wie du im Englischen wiedergeben kannst, was dir jemand anders erzählt hat (und auch, was er oder sie dich gefragt oder wozu die Person dich aufgefordert hat). Dabei verändern sich unter Umständen nicht nur die Verbformen, sondern auch die Personalpronomen und die Zeit- und Ortsangaben.

So funktioniert der Abschlusstest online:
Um deinen Lernerfolg zu überprüfen, kannst du nun die Abschlusstests machen. Gehe auf
https://www.klett-lerntraining.de/5N5D
und wähle das Kapitel und einen Test aus.

Welche Tests es gibt, siehst du unten in der Tabelle. Nach jedem Test bekommst du eine Auswertung.

Willst du immer im Blick haben, welche Themen du schon kannst oder was du besser wiederholen solltest? Dann schreibe deine Ergebnisse in die Tabelle.

Mein Ergebnis im Abschlusstest online – Kapitel 12

Thema	Mein Ergebnis
Indirekte Aussagesätze	
Zeitangaben in der indirekten Rede	
Indirekte Fragen	
Indirekte Aufforderungssätze	

Lösungen

Aufgabe 1

a) are
b) live
c) do not have/don't have (*American English*); have not got/haven't got (*British English*)
d) love
e) do not/don't like
f) is
g) owns
h) plays
i) does not/doesn't need
j) practice
k) is
l) do not/don't look
m) goes
n) has (*American English*); has got (*British English*)

Aufgabe 2

b) Do the players use a very big apple as a ball? – No, they don't.
c) Does each team want to score as many goals as possible? – Yes, it does.
d) Is a goalie's job very important? – Yes, it is.
e) Are all goalies very old? – No, they aren't.
f) Can boys play better than girls? – No, they can't.
g) Are the soccer referees' whistles very loud? – Yes, they are.
h) Does every soccer fan wear a blue scarf? – No, he/she doesn't.

Aufgabe 3

b) Where can you learn more about these rules?
c) Why does the referee need many helpers?
d) Where can you see many lines and numbers?
e) When can one team choose their side of the playing field?
f) Who is the most important player on a team?
g) Who/Whom does he lead?
h) Why do rugby balls and American footballs look alike?

Aufgabe 4

b) I am/I'm having a snowball fight. I am not/I'm not eating ice-cream.
c) She is/She's listening to an audio-book. She is not/isn't dancing in an open-air club.
d) We are/We're drinking hot tea. We are not/aren't picking fresh fruit.
e) You are/You're snowboarding. You are not/aren't sleeping in the sun.
f) He is/He's sitting in front of an open fire. He is not/isn't having a barbecue.

Aufgabe 5

b) Emma is flying a kite. She is not/isn't surfing the Internet.
c) Mr Sportslover is sailing his boat. He is not/isn't making a phone call.
d) Jacob is climbing a rock. He is not/isn't running after his sister.
e) Emma and Jacob are practicing inline skating. They are not/aren't doing their homework.
f) Mrs Sportslover is taking a break. She is not/isn't preparing dinner.

Aufgabe 6

b) Is Emma flying a kite? Yes, she is. Is she surfing the Internet? No, she is not/isn't.
c) Is Mr Sportslover sailing his boat? Yes, he is. Is he making a phone call? No, he is not/isn't.
d) Is Jacob climbing a rock? Yes, he is. Is he running after his sister? No, he is not/isn't.
e) Are Emma and Jacob practicing inline skating? Yes, they are. Are they doing their homework? No, they are not/aren't.
f) Is Mrs Sportslover taking a break? Yes, she is. Is she preparing dinner? No, she is not/isn't.

Aufgabe 7

b) Who is crying loudly in his father's arms?
c) Where is the young man preparing burgers?
d) Who is washing the dishes?
e) Why are the boy and his sister having an argument?
f) When is the manager giving change to a guest?
g) What is the young woman cleaning?
h) Why is the family ordering ice-cold drinks?

Aufgabe 8

a) What **is** she **putting** into the salad?
b) Where **is** he **getting** the ketchup?
c) How **is** he **ordering** his lunch?
d) When **are** they **bringing** me my fries?
e) Why **is** she **adding** salt to her soft drink?
f) When **are** they **having** their chocolate muffins?
g) How **is** he **talking** to the guests?
h) Why **are** they **leaving** so much trash on the table?

Aufgabe 9

a) is raining
b) are playing
c) like
d) is
e) must
f) want
g) is fighting
h) has (*American English*); has got (*British English*)
i) is losing
j) hates
k) wants
l) cannot/can't

Aufgabe 10

a) are
b) are running
c) sleeps
d) is dancing
e) can
f) is trying
g) is now chasing
h) play
i) like
j) are not eating/aren't eating
k) are throwing

Aufgabe 1

J	E	V	A	H	G	B	P
A	H	C	J	O	H	E	D
S	C	E	D	N	E	P	S
B	T	B	K	J	I	W	G
E	A	Q	E	A	W	Z	E
K	C	R	O	G	M	C	T
A	H	C	F	S	I	K	U
T	L	F	T	A	E	N	P

b) took

c) began

d) were

e) had/ate

f) had/ate

g) went

h) caught

i) made

i) spent

Aufgabe 2

1. win – lose/won – lost
2. remember – forget/remembered – forgot
3. give – keep/gave – kept
4. find – hide/found – hid
5. come – leave/came – left

Aufgabe 3

a) did not/didn't wear

b) wore

c) did not/didn't earn

d) earned

e) weren't/were not

f) was

g) sold

h) did not/didn't sell

Aufgabe 4

a) flew

b) wanted

c) did not/didn't understand

d) felt

e) visited

f) were not/weren't

g) was

h) did not/didn't meet

i) did not/didn't talk

j) learned

Aufgabe 5

b) **Did you buy** any souvenirs? – No, **I/we did not/didn't**.
c) **Did you see** a stuntman? – Yes, **I/we did.**
d) **Did he perform** any stunts for you and the other visitors? – Yes, **he did.**
e) **Did your parents take** any pictures at the studios? – No, **they did not/didn't**.
f) **Did you all** enjoy the tour? – Yes, **we did**.

Aufgabe 6

a) Why **did** you **leave** the party later than your brother?
b) What **did** you **drink** at that party?
c) Why **did** you **wear** such a short skirt?
d) Why **did you not/didn't you call** us from the party?
e) How **did** you **get** home in the middle of the night?

Aufgabe 7

b) A young woman was juggling balls. She was not/wasn't taking a dog for a walk.
c) A young man was blowing fire. He was not/wasn't going shopping.
d) A street musician was playing the guitar. He/She was not/wasn't holding an umbrella.
e) A comedian was telling jokes. He/She was not/wasn't taking notes.
f) Two boys were breakdancing. They were not/weren't wearing goggles.

Aufgabe 8

b) Was the young woman juggling balls? Yes, she was.
Was she taking a dog for a walk? No, she was not/wasn't.
c) Was the young man blowing fire? Yes, he was.
Was he going shopping? No, he was not/wasn't.
d) Was the street musician playing the guitar? Yes, he/she was.
Was he/she holding an umbrella? No, he/she was not/wasn't.
e) Was the comedian telling jokes? Yes, he/she was.
Was he/she taking notes? No, he/she was not/wasn't.
f) Were the two boys breakdancing? Yes, they were.
Were they wearing goggles? No, they were not/weren't.

Aufgabe 9

a) was reading	b) were painting
c) was watching	d) was chatting
e) was doing	f) were selling
g) was playing	h) were looking
i) was stealing	j) was sitting

Aufgabe 10

b) Who was painting graffiti on a wall?
c) Where was the policeman watching the crowd?
d) Why was I chatting to the surfing instructor?
e) What was the boy doing on his skateboard?
f) Who was selling colorful jewelry?
g) Where was the street musician playing for money?
h) Where were you looking for a place to sit?
i) What was the pickpocket stealing?
j) Why was the dog sitting in the shade?

Aufgabe 11

a) While **Emma's teacher was writing** a few grammar rules on the board …
b) … **only some of the students were copying** the rules into their exercise books.
c) What **were all the other students doing**?
d) How **were they spending** their time?
e) Why **were Cathy and Zoey not listening / weren't Cathy and Zoey listening** to the teacher's explanations?
f) They **were having** an argument.
g) **Was Josh using** his cell phone?
h) Yes, he **was texting** his girlfriend.
i) Why **was Miles crawling** under his desk?
j) He **was looking** for his pen.

Aufgabe 12

a) happened
b) was just having
c) heard
d) quickly went
e) was already waiting
f) was enjoying
g) was
h) took
i) arrived
j) was offering
k) were trying
l) managed

Aufgabe 13

a) When **did the little turtle disappear**, Mia?

b) **It was sitting** on my desk during the English test before the lunch break.

c) When **the test was** over, …

d) … **I put** it back into my bag.

e) Then **I went** to the school cafeteria …

f) … and **left** my bag in the classroom.

g) **Was anybody staying** in the classroom during the lunch break?

h) Yes, Ava and Grace **were listening** to music on Ava's cell phone.

i) And Anthony **was sleeping** at his desk, I think.

j) So he **could not/couldn't** see …

k) …who **was doing** what.

Aufgabe 1

a) has just chosen
b) has already got (*British English*); has already gotten (*American English*)
c) have never had
d) have just found
e) have never lost
f) have already sorted out

Aufgabe 2

b) Have the students already made all the posters for the school hall?
No, they have not/haven't made all the posters for the school hall yet.
c) Has the headmaster already written down the program?
No, he/she has not/hasn't written down the program yet.
d) Has the janitor already repaired all the broken chairs?
No, he/she has not/hasn't repaired all the broken chairs yet.
e) Has the school secretary already sent invitations to all students' families? –
No, he/she has not/hasn't sent invitations to all students' families yet.
f) Have the teachers already finished all the class projects?
No, they have not/haven't finished all the class projects yet.

Aufgabe 3

a) The Sportslovers are really lucky. What **has happened**?
b) They **have just bought** tickets to a basketball game to see their favorite team.
c) **Have they ever seen** a game with this team before? – Yes, **they have**.
d) **Have they ever worn** their fan shirts before? – No, **they have not/haven't**.
e) **Have they already sat** down in the stadium? – No, **they have not/haven't**.
f) Why **have they not found/haven't they found** their seats yet?
g) **Have they got** lost in the stadium? (British English)
Have they gotten lost in the stadium? (American English) – No, **they have not/haven't**.
h) They **have just had** an interesting conversation.
i) Who **have they just** talked to?
j) They **have just spoken with** the team's captain.

Aufgabe 4

a) have been waiting
b) has been ringing
c) has been trying
d) have been looking
e) has been running
f) has been listening

Aufgabe 5

Die Zeitangaben kannst du in beliebiger Reihenfolge verwenden.

a) have been trying
b) have not/haven't been looking
c) have been dancing
d) have been dreaming
e) have been thinking
f) have been admiring
g) You have been standing
h) have been searching

Aufgabe 6

a) What **have Emma and Alec been doing** all evening?
b) Where **have they been spending** their time together?
c) **Have they been walking** along the beach? – No, they **have not/haven't**.
d) **Have they been looking** at the stars? – No, they **have not/haven't**.
e) **Have they been watching** a movie? – No, they **have not/haven't**.
f) They **have been spending** their time at a shopping mall.
g) **Has Alec been holding** Emma's hand? – No, he **has not/hasn't**.
h) **He has been carrying** around his laptop and a bottle of coke.
i) What **have Emma and Alec been talking** about for the last hour?
j) Alec **has been telling** Emma jokes which aren't funny.

Aufgabe 7

a) **since** last Monday
b) **since** yesterday
c) **for** twenty minutes
d) **for** my whole life
e) **for** a couple of weeks
f) **for** a few months
g) **since** the year 2012
h) **since** I was born

Aufgabe 8

a) has been waiting; sent
b) hasn't arrived; phoned
c) has been trying; got up
d) hasn't heard; met
e) hasn't got; ordered
f) has been standing; started

Aufgabe 9

a) began/started
b) has been going on
c) have already scored
d) played
e) has been

Aufgabe 10

a) sent
b) has been
c) landed
d) have been dreaming
e) have done / have been doing
f) have not/haven't discovered
g) have been playing
h) have not/haven't only used
i) have also helped / have also been helping
j) imagined

Aufgabe 1

a) had surprised
b) had invited
c) had done all
d) had bought
e) had carried
f) had hung up
g) had prepared

Aufgabe 2

a) had not/hadn't put
b) had put
c) had not/hadn't left
d) had left
e) had not/hadn't taken
f) had taken
g) had not/hadn't packed
h) had packed
i) had not/hadn't thrown
j) had thrown
k) had not/hadn't hidden
l) had hidden

Aufgabe 3

a) had discovered
b) Had she also discovered – had not/hadn't
c) had built
d) had not/hadn't built
e) had developed
f) had invented
e) Had he also invented – had not/hadn't

Aufgabe 4

a) Who had been able to imagine the great success of the Internet (before it became popular in the 1990s)?
b) Why had scientists tested a new communication system (before 1969)?
c) Who(m) had the Internet helped to communicate secretly?
d) Who had spent many years of research on it?
e) What had failed many times before the scientists were finally successful?

Aufgabe 5

a) had been repeating
b) had been practicing
c) had been doing
d) had been talking
e) had been bragging
f) had been scaring

Aufgabe 6

b) The surfing instructor had been giving lessons. He/She had not/hadn't been relaxing on the beach.
c) The janitor had been painting the walls. He/She had not/hadn't been repairing the door.
d) The journalist had been working on an article. He/She had not/hadn't been taking pictures.
e) The tourist guide had been talking about the sights. He/She had not/hadn't been sitting in a café.
f) The student had been doing grammar exercises. He/She had not/hadn't been sleeping.

Aufgabe 7

b) Had the surfing instructor been giving lessons? – Yes, he/she had.
Had he/she been relaxing on the beach? – No, he/she had not/hadn't.

c) Had the janitor been painting the walls? – Yes, he/she had.
Had he/she been repairing the door? – No, he/she had not/hadn't.

d) Had the journalist been working on an article? – Yes, he/she had.
Had he/she been taking pictures? – No, he/she had not/hadn't.

e) Had the tourist guide been talking about the sights? – Yes, he/she had.
Had he/she been sitting in a café? – No, he/she had not/hadn't.

f) Had the student been doing grammar exercises? – Yes, he/she had.
Had he/she been sleeping? – No, he/she had not/hadn't.

Aufgabe 8

a) How long **had the candidates been waiting** before the show began?
b) They **had been waiting** since early morning.
c) What **had they been showing** when the audience clapped?
d) They **had been showing** their talents.
e) Why **had the judges been staring** at one of the candidates before they made their decision?
f) They **had been staring** at her because of her brilliant performance.
g) How long **had the judges been discussing** the candidates' performances until they decided on a winner?
h) They **had been discussing** for half an hour.
i) Why **had the winner of the show been crying** before the show ended?
j) She **had been crying** for joy.

Aufgabe 9

a) had been thinking
b) had had
c) had been walking
d) had been looking
e) had tried
f) had asked
g) had been saving
h) had put on

Aufgabe 10

a) had been waiting; arrived
b) had bought; went
c) had already heard; decided
d) had been looking; discovered
e) had; had made
f) took; had locked
g) had been standing; was

Aufgabe 1

a) will be
b) will need
c) will not/won't see
d) will make
e) will give
f) will not/won't rain
g) will bring
h) will not/won't rise

Aufgabe 2

b) Will racing cars soon go faster than 500 km/h? – Yes, they will./No, they will not/won't.
c) Will handball become more popular than soccer? – Yes, it will./No, it will not/won't.
d) Will German schools offer their students skateboarding instead of normal sports classes? – Yes, they will./No, they will not/won't.
e) Will Olympic Games still exist in fifty years? – Yes, they will./No, they will not/won't.
f) Will German soccer players play like Brazilians one day? – Yes, they will./No, they will not/won't.

Aufgabe 3

a) Who will be the next President of the USA?
b) When will American scientists invent the next big thing?
c) Who will win the next film award?
d) When will the next snowstorm hit California?
e) How many people will live in the USA in twenty years?
f) What will be the title of the next number one song?

Aufgabe 4

a) Will you tell
b) I will inform
c) Will five dollars be
d) my answers will be
e) will I do
f) You will become
g) will I live
h) You will own
i) Will I have
j) You will be
k) Will I be
l) You will get

Aufgabe 5

a) are going to visit
b) are going to spend
c) are going to have
d) are going to buy
e) are going to fly
f) are going to listen
g) are going to see
h) are going to take

Aufgabe 6

a) is going to stop
b) are going to eat
c) is going to work
d) am not/I'm not going to watch
e) are going to do
f) is going to go
g) are not/aren't going to drink
h) is going to learn
i) is not/isn't going to get up
j) am not/I'm not going to spend

Aufgabe 7

a) When **are** you **going to do** your homework?

b) Who **are** you **going to meet** tonight?

c) Where **are** you **going to go** next?

d) When **are** you **going to clean up** your room?

e) What **are** you **going to do** about your grades?

Aufgabe 8

a) What **are they going to do** now?

b) **Are they going to buy** a new car? No, they **are not/aren't**.

c) Dad **is going to repair** the old one.

d) Where **is she going to look for** it?

e) She **is going to search for** a similar recipe on the Internet.

f) Then she **is going to bake** Emma's birthday cake.

g) **Is he going to go** back home and get it? – No, he **is not/isn't**.

h) He **is going to call** his parents on his cell phone …

i) … and then **he is going to ask** them what to buy at the supermarket.

Aufgabe 9

a) starts
b) are going to start
c) will start
d) is going to open
e) won't open
f) will open
g) are going
h) Are they going to go
i) will go

Aufgabe 10

a) are giving
b) will take off
c) is going to shine
d) won't be
e) are going to check
f) are going to say
g) will be
h) starts

Aufgabe 11

a) ~~drives~~ / is driving
b) leaves / ~~will leave~~
c) will last / ~~is lasting~~
d) is going to read / ~~will read~~
e) lands / ~~is going to land~~
f) ~~are taking~~ / are going to take
g) won't be / ~~isn't going to be~~
h) ~~aren't spending~~ / won't spend
i) are going to do / ~~will do~~
j) is / ~~will be~~
k) ~~is going to call~~ / will call
l) ~~are visiting~~/will visit

Aufgabe 1

b) Tourists must always stay on the trails.
c) They must not/mustn't feed bears or other wild animals.
d) They must not/mustn't use bicycles on the trails.
e) They must keep away from the icy river.
f) They can fish here only with a fishing license.

Aufgabe 2

b) Tourists always have to stay on the trails.
c) They are not/aren't allowed to feed bears or other wild animals.
d) They are not/aren't allowed to use bicycles on the trails.
e) They have to keep away from the icy river.
f) They are allowed to fish here only with a fishing license.

Aufgabe 3

a) can/are allowed to
b) can/may/ are allowed to
c) need not/needn't/do not have to/don't have to
d) must/have to
e) can/are able to
f) must not/mustn't
g) cannot/can't
h) must/have to
i) cannot/can't
j) need not/needn't/do not have to/don't have to

Aufgabe 4

b) They **were allowed to** stay there for a couple of days.
c) They **did not have to/didn't have to** take their parents with them.
d) At the camp they **had to** get up very early.
e) The climbers there **were able to** teach each other different climbing techniques.
f) The most important rule was that they **were not/weren't allowed to** climb alone.
g) The teenagers at the camp **were not/weren't able to** hang out much …
h) … because they **had to** do a lot of sports.
i) There was no electricity at the camp, so the young climbers **were not/weren't able to** watch TV in the evenings.
j) But at least they **did not/didn't have to** do schoolwork while they were at the camp.

Aufgabe 5

a) have not/haven't been allowed to
b) have not/haven't been able to
c) was able to
d) have been allowed to
e) had to
f) will soon be allowed to
g) is allowed to
h) were not/weren't allowed to
i) have had to

Aufgabe 6

a) were allowed to
b) had not/hadn't been allowed to
c) were able to
d) had been able to
e) have been allowed to
f) had had to
g) was able to
h) had already been able to
i) were not/weren't able to
j) have had to

Aufgabe 7

a) You must have heard of that new TV show.
b) I shouldn't have watched that horror movie.
c) He needn't have recorded the live concert.
d) We might have laughed about that comedian.
e) They couldn't have imagined a more exciting thriller.

Aufgabe 8

b) The goalie should have stopped the ball.
c) The cyclist should have exercised more.
d) The referee must/might have made an unfair decision.
e) The basketball player should have jumped higher.
f) The swimmer needn't/shouldn't have worried about the competition.
g) The mountain biker should have worn a helmet.
h) The runner should have thought of wearing running shoes.
i) The surfer needn't have put on sunscreen.

Aufgabe 9

b) He **should have/could have been** more careful.
c) They **need not/needn't/should not/shouldn't have bought** so much meat.
d) She **should have/could have looked after** her things better.
e) The young man **need not/needn't have taken** his own food with him.
f) He **should have/could have come** earlier.
g) Somebody **must have left** it there.
h) They **should have/could have checked** the number of beds more carefully.

Aufgabe 1

Es sind alle Kombinationen möglich. Entscheidend ist die richtige Form des *gerund*:

a) Bowling
b) Surfing
c) Talking
d) Playing
e) Solving
f) Listening
g) Acting
h) Looking
i) Reading
j) Collecting

Aufgabe 2

a) Chatting
b) Drinking
c) Staying
d) Playing
e) Smoking

Aufgabe 3

a) to finishing
b) like closing
c) of studying
d) of doing
e) about spending
f) on improving

Aufgabe 4

a) idea of travelling (*British English*); idea of traveling (*American English*)
b) interested in learning
c) tired of experiencing
d) good at making
e) chance of becoming
f) crazy about doing
g) afraid of having
h) used to working out

Aufgabe 5

a) going Infinitiv: ☐ möglich ☒ nicht möglich
b) sending Infinitiv: ☒ möglich ☐ nicht möglich
c) teaching Infinitiv: ☒ möglich ☐ nicht möglich
d) taking Infinitiv: ☒ möglich ☐ nicht möglich
e) missing Infinitiv: ☐ möglich ☒ nicht möglich
f) studying Infinitiv: ☐ möglich ☒ nicht möglich
g) having Infinitiv: ☐ möglich ☒ nicht möglich

Aufgabe 6

a) getting away
b) continuing/to continue
c) to stay
d) to live
e) spending/to spend
f) thinking/to think
g) to enjoy

Aufgabe 7

a) talking
b) meeting
c) to switch
d) playing
e) to leave
f) beginning
g) thinking
h) offering
i) to let
j) to say

Aufgabe 1

b) I expect you **to listen to the noises of nocturnal animals**.
c) I don't want you **to laugh or scream loudly**.
d) I expect you never **to leave the trail on your own**.
e) I don't want you **to pick any wild flowers**.
f) I want all of you **to wear warm jackets and sturdy boots**.
g) I don't want you **to use your cell phones unless there is an emergency**.

Aufgabe 2

Hier sind natürlich auch andere Satzeinleitungen möglich.
b) He asks them not to lean out of the windows.
c) He would like them not to leave any garbage on the seats.
d) He doesn't want them to get on other passengers' nerves.
e) He expects them not to pull the emergency brake.
f) He doesn't want them to eat burgers or ice-cream on the train.
g) He advises them to keep their voices down.

Aufgabe 3

Die Einleitungsverben kannst du in den einzelnen Sätzen beliebig austauschen.
a) Lena wonders how to get to the beach.
b) She doesn't know what to do on a rainy day.
c) She has no idea how/where to find the best burgers.
d) She isn't sure how/where to meet celebs.
e) She wonders where to buy cheap fashion.
f) She doesn't know what to expect from her vacation.

Aufgabe 4

b) They wonder **which terminal to go to**.
c) They aren't sure **when to check in**.
d) They have no idea **what to put into their hand luggage**.
e) They don't know **what not to wear for the security check**.
f) They aren't sure **how long to wait for boarding**.

Aufgabe 5

Du kannst jeweils auch andere einleitende Verben verwenden.

b) The traveler wondered who to ask for information about the departure of his/her flight.
c) He wanted to know where to report a theft.
d) She did not/didn't know how to get to the viewing platform.
e) The traveler was not/wasn't sure what to do if he/she had missed his/her flight.
f) She wondered where to buy duty free perfume.
g) He wanted to know what to do to get his lost luggage back.
h) She had no idea where to go to find a doctor.

Aufgabe 6

Es sind auch andere Kombinationen möglich als die hier angegebenen.

a) Dad was the first to hear the alarm clock.
b) Jacob wasn't the first to get dressed.
c) Mom wasn't the only one to set the table for breakfast.
d) Emma was the only one to do a few sit-ups.
e) Mom was the last to leave the house.

Aufgabe 7

b) He is always **the first to cross the finish line.**
c) She will be **the youngest girl to graduate from Jacob's school.**
d) She is **the most realistic person to talk to.**
e) He is **the only student to work patiently on difficult problems.**
f) He is **the most open student to talk to.**
g) She is always **the last to finish lunch.**
h) He is **the most aggressive boy to have an argument with.**
i) She is **the only student to tell really funny jokes.**

Aufgabe 1

a) First you need two slices of white bread.
Two slices of white bread are needed.

b) You put a little mayonnaise onto one slice of bread.
A little mayonnaise is put onto one slice of bread.

c) You lay some bacon on it.
Some bacon is laid on it.

d) You add some lettuce and some tomato slices.
Some lettuce and some tomato slices are added.

e) You top all that with the second slice of bread.
All that is topped with the second slice of bread.

f) You cut the sandwich into four pieces.
The sandwich is cut into four pieces.

g) You eat the sandwich with some potato chips.
The sandwich is eaten with some potato chips.

Aufgabe 2

a) was entered
b) were opened
c) were hidden
d) were put
e) were covered
f) were left

Aufgabe 3

b) The food for the buffet **has already been ordered**.
c) The red carpet **has already been laid down**.
d) The press conference **has not/hasn't been held yet**.
e) 200 bottles of champagne **have already been bought**.
f) The speeches about the winners of the awards **have not/haven't been written yet**.

Aufgabe 4

a) was discovered
b) was seen
c) had been told
d) was found
e) were brought

Aufgabe 5

a) will be built
b) will not/won't be used
c) will be seen
d) will be planted
e) will be kept

Aufgabe 6

a) Many visitors are attracted by the Walk of Fame in Hollywood every year.
b) That famous sight is formed by more than 2,000 stars on the sidewalk.
c) After the idea for the Walk of Fame had been discussed by some business people in the 1950s …
d) … the situation was made difficult for them by money problems.
e) The first stars with artists' names were finished in 1960.
f) More than 2,000 stars have been added since then.
g) Many more artists will be honored with a star in the next century.

Aufgabe 7

a) is often said / has often been said
b) is simply called
c) was made
d) had been founded
e) was bought
f) has been known
g) was reported
h) has been done
i) will always be loved

Aufgabe 8

b) A director is being interviewed.
c) Articles are being written.
d) Costumes are being made.
e) Tickets are being sold.
f) A movie is being shot.
g) A movie studio is being opened.
h) Ideas are being discussed.

Aufgabe 9

a) is usually played
b) is shared
c) are set up
d) is chosen
e) is rolled
f) is being done
g) are being scored
h) are always counted
i) are just being shown
j) is being cheered on

Aufgabe 10

a) were being painted
b) were being changed
c) was being laid
d) were being cleaned
e) were being carried
f) were being set up

Aufgabe 11

a) are being offered
b) were being sold
c) were being advertised
d) are being shown
e) are being put
f) were being presented

Aufgabe 12

a) was watched
b) were flown
c) were being filmed
d) were being watched
e) were placed
f) were built
g) was prepared
h) were being collected
i) were being cooked
j) were confronted
k) were chosen
l) was given

Aufgabe 13

Es sind auch andere Kombinationen als angegeben möglich. Entscheidend ist die richtige Konstruktion mit dem Infinitiv Passiv.

b) Viewers hope **to be informed** about important events.
c) They want **to be entertained** by a romantic comedy.
d) People would like **to be shown** high-quality documentaries.
e) Viewers wish **to be told** about politics.
f) They hope **to be informed** about the economic situation.
g) People wish **to be entertained** by funny cartoons.
h) Viewers would like **to be shown** thrillers.

Aufgabe 14

b) They hope to be praised by the judges.
c) They expect to be given a new look by the hair stylists.
d) They hope to be dressed in expensive clothes by famous designers.
e) They wish to be flown to exotic places by the TV station.
f) They expect to be photographed by professionals.
g) They wish to be admired by the viewers.
h) They hope to be chosen to be on the cover by a fashion magazine.
i) They hope to be offered a contract by a good modeling agency.
j) They expect to be given the first prize by the judges.

Aufgabe 15

b) Everything must be/should be/ought to be left the way you found it.
c) Nothing must/should be cleaned.
d) A room must not be/mustn't be/should not be/shouldn't be/ought not to be entered if …
e) A list of the precious things in your house must be/should be/ought to be written.

Aufgabe 16

b) The grass must be/should be/ought to be cut.
c) The cat must be/should be/ought to be fed.
d) The windows must be/should be/ought to be opened and closed again.
e) The mailbox must be/should be/ought to be checked.
f) The dog must be/should be/ought to be walked.

Aufgabe 17

b) Mom and Dad have been promised help at home and in the garden.
Help at home and in the garden has been promised to Mom and Dad.
c) The Sportslovers have been sent four vouchers for sportswear.
Four vouchers for sportswear have been sent to the Sportslovers.
d) The family has been lent a camper van.
A camper van has been lent to the family.
e) Jacob has been sold an unused tent at a very good price.
An unused tent has been sold at a very good price to Jacob.
f) Emma and Jacob have been shown a special place at the beach.
A special place at the beach has been shown to Emma and Jacob.

Aufgabe 18

b) Emma's friend sends her an e-mail with a computer virus.
Emma is sent an e-mail with a computer virus.
c) Jacob's classmate tells Emma one of Jacob's secrets.
Emma is told one of Jacob's secrets.
d) A travel company offers the Sportslovers a vacation at a hotel that doesn't exist.
The Sportslovers are offered a vacation at a hotel that doesn't exist.
e) A friend lends Emma a pair of broken ice skates.
Emma is lent a pair of broken ice skates.
f) A neighbor writes the Sportslovers letters of complaint.
The Sportslovers are written letters of complaint.

Aufgabe 19

b) We **promise** you weeks full of fun activities.
You **are promised** weeks full of fun activities.

c) Our sports camp **gives/offers** you a chance to meet interesting people from all over the world.
You **are given/are offered** a chance to meet interesting people from all over the world.

d) Our hotel **offers** all hobby surfers many great activities.
All hobby surfers **are offered** many great activities.

e) The world's best surfers **will show/will teach** you useful tricks.
You **will be shown/will be taught** useful tricks by the world's best surfers.

f) They **will tell** you about the secrets of surfing well during the daily lessons.
You **will be told** about the secrets of surfing well during the daily lessons.

g) The experts on our hotline **will tell** you more about the whole travel package.
You **will be told** more about the whole travel package by the experts on our hotline.

h) They **will tell** you all about our prices and conditions.
You **will be told** all about our prices and conditions.

i) They **will send** you our brochure with all the necessary information.
You **will be sent** our brochure with all the necessary information.

Aufgabe 1

a) Hollywood; which/that
b) Mississippi; which/that
c) White House; which/that
d) George Washington; who/that
e) Madonna; who/that

Aufgabe 2

a) The person **who/that** makes sure that a soccer game is fair is called a referee.
contact clause: ☐ möglich ☒ nicht möglich

b) The special glasses **which/that** you wear in the swimming pool are called goggles.
contact clause: ☒ möglich ☐ nicht möglich

c) The thing **which/that** you hit the tennis ball with is called a racket.
contact clause: ☒ möglich ☐ nicht möglich

d) Someone **who/that** uses a board with four small wheels to do tricks in the air is called a skater.
contact clause: ☐ möglich ☒ nicht möglich

e) The prize **which/that** you can win at the Olympics is called a medal.
contact clause: ☒ möglich ☐ nicht möglich

Aufgabe 3

a) 4. California is a state <u>whose climate is very warm</u>.
b) 1. A famous Californian <u>whose career started in the 1970s</u> is Arnold Schwarzenegger.
c) 2. Many scientists <u>whose main interest is computers</u> work in Silicon Valley.
d) 3. Many tourists <u>whose hobby is surfing</u> come to California.

Aufgabe 4

b) The man whose left eye is covered by a patch is very tall.
c) The woman who/that helped the man had a gun.
d) The passport (which/that) the woman lost in the bank is fake.
e) The person who/that was behind the wheel of the getaway car wore a black mask.
f) The sports bag (which/that) the robbers used to carry the money out of the bank was red and white.
g) The robbery happened in a bank whose clients are mostly rich.

Aufgabe 5

a) A pencil case is a kind of small bag (**that/which**) you keep your pens and pencils in.
b) A guidance teacher is a person (**that/who**) you can talk to in difficult situations.
c) A board is a large object (**that/which**) the teacher writes on during lessons.
d) The student (**that/who**) you sit next to in the English lessons is your classmate.

Aufgabe 6

b) You can buy a pair of soccer shoes a world champion practiced in.
c) You can find a house a film star lived in.
d) You can buy a cup a pop singer drank from.
e) You can find a bag the President's wife showed up with.
f) You can buy a pen a famous author wrote with.
g) You can find a book a princess drew a picture in.

Aufgabe 7

b) The shop assistant with whom I am angry is not here today.
c) The product about which I want to complain is your chocolate.
d) The shop assistant from whom I bought it had recommended the chocolate to me.
e) The problem about which I would like to talk is that your chocolate is of very low quality.

Aufgabe 8

a) Las Vegas, **which** is the biggest city in Nevada, is well-known for its casinos.
b) It is a place (**which/that**) millions of tourists visit every year.
c) The tourists often go to one of the many shows (**which/that**) you can see there.
d) Elvis Presley, **who** performed in Las Vegas for several years, is still alive there.
e) There are many actors and singers **who/that** dress up as Elvis.
f) Maybe you have heard of the artists Siegfried and Roy, **who** both come from Germany.
g) They worked with white tigers, **which** are very beautiful but can also be very aggressive.
h) In a show a couple of years ago a tiger attacked Roy, **whose** throat was hurt very badly.
i) The wedding chapels of Las Vegas, **which** are a reason for many couples to come, are famous all over the world.
j) Couples **who/that** want to marry can do it very quickly there.
k) You can't imagine all the costumes and decorations (**which/that**) they can choose from.

Aufgabe 9

b) A fact (which/that) many people don't know is that "D.C." is short for "District of Columbia".
c) About 600,000 people live in Washington, which is also the seat of the American government.
d) You may have seen a picture of the Capitol, which is a very famous building.
e) The city was named after the first President of the USA, who was called George Washington.

Aufgabe 10

a) There is a lot of rain in Washington, a city **whose** climate isn't very mild.
b) The people **who/that** founded Washington settled close to the Potomac River.
c) A building (**which/that**) many people want to see in Washington is the White House.

Aufgabe 1

b) If you **share** these chocolate bars with your friends, you **will have** lots of fun.
c) If you **wear** these jeans, you **will look** like a rock star.
d) If you **drink** a cup of this tea, you **will feel** relaxed.
e) If you **use** this shower gel, you **will smell** like a rose.
f) If you **have** this drink, you **will feel** a lot more energetic.

Aufgabe 2

a) 6. If people only **read** e-books, they **won't need** book shelves anymore.
b) 1. If robots **can answer** all your questions, they **will be able to have** long conversations with you.
c) 5. If computers **can drive** your car, you **will be able to sleep** behind the wheel.
d) 2. If everybody **pays** for everything by credit card, there **will be** no more coins.
e) 4. If you **can scan** all the products at the supermarket yourself, nobody **will work** at the check-out counter anymore.
f) 3. If people **write** everything using computer keyboards, they **will forget** how to write by hand.

Aufgabe 3

b) If you **dream** of being famous, **take part / you should take part** in a casting show.
c) If your best friend **hurts** you, **tell / you should tell** him (her) how you feel.
d) If you always **get up** too late, **put / you should put** a second alarm clock next to your bed.
e) If your room **looks** too boring, **hang up / you should hang up** some colorful posters.
f) If you always **fight** with your family over which TV show to watch, **let / you should let** each family member pick one show a week.
g) If your teacher **is** always grumpy, **ask / you should ask** him (her) about the reason.

Aufgabe 4

a) when b) When c) If d) if

Aufgabe 5

a) When; arrive; will try
b) If; is; will go
c) When; go; will watch out
d) can take; if; are
e) If; see; will stand
f) If; takes away; will not/won't try
g) When; pack; must remember
h) can; when; walk

Aufgabe 6

b) If I was a pilot, I would/could see the whole world.
c) If I was a cowboy/cowgirl, I would/could spend the whole day on horseback.
d) If I was a scientist, I would/could invent a robot that does my homework.
e) If I was a teacher, I would/could never shout at my students.
f) If I was a manager, I would/could work in an office in a skyscraper.

Aufgabe 7

a) had; would walk
b) would be; could play
c) would learn; did not/didn't work
d) owned; would sail

Aufgabe 8

b) If my parents read the text messages on my mobile phone, I wouldn't/would accept it. I would/wouldn't start an argument.
c) If my classmates said bad things about my best friend, I would/wouldn't tell him / her. I would/wouldn't keep the whole thing to myself.
d) If my teacher treated my classmate unfairly, I would/wouldn't speak up for him/her. I wouldn't/would keep quiet.
e) If I was/were late for school simply because I had been walking too slowly, I wouldn't/would tell the teacher the truth. I would/wouldn't tell him/her a lie.
f) If my parents were away over the week-end, I wouldn't/would study for my English test. I would/wouldn't have a party.
g) If I got a text message from a secret admirer, I would/wouldn't want to find out who he/she is. I wouldn't/would forget about it.
h) If my neighbor was very good at English, I wouldn't/would copy from him/her while taking a test. I would/wouldn't write down my own ideas.

Aufgabe 9

a) If it wasn't seven o'clock, Emma wouldn't get up.
b) If the cake is good, Jacob will eat another piece.
c) If Jacob wasn't such a good runner, he wouldn't win the race.
d) If Emma doesn't catch the bus, she will wait for the next one.
e) If Emma was at the beach, she would go for a swim.

Aufgabe 10

a) If John Supersurf **had listened** to his friends, he **would have stayed** at home on that stormy day.

b) If he **had not/hadn't tried** to surf, he **would not/wouldn't have had** that terrible accident.

c) John **would not/wouldn't have fallen** off his surfboard if he **had not/hadn't been** so tired.

d) If there **had not/hadn't been** such high waves, John **would not/wouldn't have hit** his head on the board.

e) If he **had not/hadn't lost** any blood, the shark **would not/wouldn't have smelled** it.

f) If the shark **had not/hadn't found** John, it **would not/wouldn't have attacked** him.

g) If John's friends **had not/hadn't worried** about him, they **would not/wouldn't have called** the coast guard.

h) John would **not/wouldn't have survived** if the coast guard **had not/hadn't saved** him.

i) If a journalist **had not/hadn't heard** about that story, she **would not/wouldn't have written** an article about it.

Aufgabe 11

b) If Emma had gone slower, she would not/wouldn't have fallen down in the street.

c) If Mr Sportslover gets as many mails as yesterday, it will take him the whole afternoon to read them.

d) If Mrs Sportslover gets home in time, she will/can watch her favorite soap on TV.

e) If Jacob was not/wasn't her brother, Emma would not/wouldn't lend him her new jacket.

f) If Jacob had prepared better for the test, he would have had a better grade.

Aufgabe 1

Die einleitenden Verben können auch in anderer Reihenfolge verwendet werden.

b) He adds (that) he comes from a small town near Frankfurt.
c) He explains (that) he has been learning English for four years.
d) He tells the students (that) before he came here on the exchange …
e) … he had never been to the USA.
f) He mentions (that) he has already learned a lot about California.
g) He explains (that) he really loves the American way of life.
h) He hopes (that) he will come back to LA one day.

Aufgabe 2

Die einleitenden Verben können auch in anderer Reihenfolge verwendet werden.

b) He added (that) he came from a small town near Frankfurt.
c) He explained (that) he had been learning English for four years.
d) He told the students (that) before he had come here with the exchange …
e) … he had never been to the USA before.
f) He mentioned (that) he had already learned a lot about California.
g) He explained (that) he really loved the American way of life.
h) He hoped (that) he would come back to LA one day.

Aufgabe 3

b) She added (that) he had wanted to play with Luke between classes.
c) She explained (that) Matt had thrown the ball at Luke.
d) She said (that) he had accidentally hit the lamp.
e) She added (that) luckily nobody had been hurt.

Aufgabe 4

Hier sind jeweils auch andere Einleitungsverben möglich.

a) Jacob said (that) he wanted to get a small tattoo on his back.
b) His mom answered (that) he was much too young to get a tattoo.
c) Jacob said (that) people who were much younger had already gotten a tattoo.
d) His mom answered (that) she did not/didn't care what other people did.
e) Jacob told his mom (that) there were simply no good reasons for her decision.
f) His mom explained (that) tattoos were bad for his health.
g) Jacob told his mom (that) the tattoo studio used only safe tattoo inks.
h) His mom said (that) if the studio was not/wasn't clean, he would still risk infections.
i) Jacob offered his mom (that) she could come with him to the studio and see if it was clean.
j) His mom answered (that) it would be difficult to get a job if he had a tattoo.
k) Jacob explained (that) nobody would see his tattoo if it was on his back.
l) His mom said (that) maybe he would not/wouldn't like the tattoo anymore when he was older.
m) Jacob told her (that) if that was the case, he could get rid of his tattoo.
n) His mom said (that) she had had enough and that she would never allow him to get a tattoo.

Aufgabe 5

Hier sind jeweils auch andere Einleitungsverben möglich.

b) He told me (that) he had gone to Venice Beach **yesterday**.
c) He added (that) **that place** was simply fantastic.
d) He explained (that) they could choose between different activities at school **today**.
e) He said (that) he had gone to American football training **this afternoon**.
f) He said (that) Jacob, a boy from school, had invited him to a barbecue party **tonight**.
g) He told me (that) he was going to stay with Jacob's family **until tomorrow**.
h) He added (that) he was going to take a diving lesson **tomorrow**.
i) He mentioned (that) he was also looking forward to going to the school dance **next week-end**.

Aufgabe 6

Hier ändern sich gegenüber Aufgabe 5 nur die Zeitangaben.

b) the day before	c) (keine Änderung)	d) that day
e) that afternoon	f) (keine Änderung)	g) that night
h) until the following day	i) the following day	j) the following week

Aufgabe 7

b) They wanted to know **if/whether he had a girlfriend.**

c) The boys and girls asked **if/whether he had ever had a date with an American girl.**

d) Jacob's classmates wanted to find out **if/whether there were any differences between Germans and Americans.**

e) They asked **if/whether he had ever been to a school dance.**

f) One of their questions was **if/whether he had seen a lot of California yet.**

g) The students were interested in finding out **if/whether he knew any Americans in Europe.**

Aufgabe 8

Hier sind jeweils auch andere Einleitungsverben möglich.

b) He wanted to know if/whether he had slept during the flight.

c) He asked if/whether he had got/had gotten a seat next to his friend on the plane.

d) He wanted to know if/whether the food on board the plane had been all right.

e) He asked if/whether the stewardess had spoken German.

f) He asked if/whether his host family had met him at the airport in LA.

g) He wanted to know if/whether he felt comfortable with his host family.

h) He asked if he was sharing a room with his host brother.

Aufgabe 9

b) Never ask where your date got his/her terrible haircut.

c) Never ask why he/she can't tell you anything more interesting.

d) Never ask when you can go home.

e) Never ask why he/she chose such a boring movie.

f) Never ask when he/she will stop getting on your nerves.

g) Never ask what you can do to finish that date as quickly as possible.

h) Never ask why you didn't say no when he/she asked you out.

Aufgabe 10

Hier sind jeweils auch andere Einleitungsverben möglich.

b) Benjamin asked Nicky where she had bought that fantastic dress.

c) He asked her what she wanted to know about him.

d) He wanted to know what she usually did on week-ends.

e) He wondered how she had learned to speak German so well.

f) He asked who(m) she hung out with at school.

g) He wanted to know what kind of movies she liked.

h) He asked her when he would see her again.

Aufgabe 11

a) "Who was driving the car at the time of the accident?"
b) "Has anybody been injured?"
c) "Why didn't you stop at the traffic light?"

Aufgabe 12

a) The teacher asked the students to show respect to their fellow classmates.
b) She advised them not to distract each other.
c) She told them not to talk if it was not/wasn't their turn.
d) She reminded them never to laugh about a wrong answer.
e) She warned them not to tell her lies about their missing homework.
f) She told them not to hit each other.
g) She asked them to keep the classroom clean and tidy.
h) She advised them not to make fun of their fellow classmates.
i) She reminded them to come to the lessons on time.
j) She warned them to turn off their cell phones during lessons.
k) She askem them not to wear caps or hats in the classroom.

Aufgabe 13

Hier darfst du natürlich in jedem Satz auch andere passende Einleitungsverben benutzen!

b) He told them to remember that many things were different in Germany.
c) He warned them to always be polite to their host families.
d) He reminded them not to behave selfishly.
e) He advised them not to break their host parents' rules.
f) He reminded them to take warm clothes with them.
g) He asked them to take part in their host families' activities.
h) He told them to bring their host families some small presents.
i) He advised them to try to speak some simple German sentences.
j) He reminded them not to forget their dictionaries.